Growth and Structure of Tertiary Sector in Developing Economies

Seema Joshi is Senior Sir Ratan Tata Fellow at Institute of Economic Growth, University of Delhi, Delhi, on deputation from the Kirori Mal College, University of Delhi, where she is Reader of Economics, Department of Commerce. Dr Joshi's areas of interest include issues related to tertiary sector, social sector and urban management. While handling various training and teaching assignments, she also designed and taught an Elective Stream "Economics of the Services Sector" for XXXII Advanced Professional Programme in Public Administration (2006-07) during her deputation to Indian Institute of Public Administration as Associate Professor of Urban Management (September 2005 to May 2007).

Growth and Structure of Tertiary Sector in Developing Economies

Seema Joshi

ACADEMIC FOUNDATION
NEW DELHI

First published in 2008
by

ACADEMIC FOUNDATION
4772-73 / 23 Bharat Ram Road, (23 Ansari Road),
Darya Ganj, New Delhi - 110 002 (India).
Phones : 23245001 / 02 / 03 / 04.
Fax : +91-11-23245005.
E-mail : academic@vsnl.com
www. academicfoundation.com

Cataloging in Publication Data--DK
Courtesy: D.K. Agencies (P) Ltd. <docinfo@dkagencies.com>

Joshi, Seema.
Growth and structure of tertiary sector in developing economies : some reflections / Seema Joshi. p. cm.
With special reference to India. Includes index.
ISBN 13: 9788171886319
ISBN 10: 8171886310

1. Service industries. 2. Service industries—India. 3. Economic development. 4. Economic development--India. I. Title.

DDC 338.470 009 54 22

Typeset by Italics India, New Delhi.
Printed and bound in India.

To
My Parents
and
My Teacher

Contents

List of Tables

Tables

Foreword

The present study was carried out with a view to examining the growth of tertiary sector *vis-à-vis* material production sectors in developing economies. It has been noticed that in most of the developing countries the services sector has been growing faster than the commodity producing sectors. And this has raised concerns from the point of view of the sustainability of growth and the implications of such kind of growth.

In this context the study by Dr. Joshi is relevant and timely. She examines the nature of growth of services in developing economies in general and India in particular. She also examines the inter-temporal changes in the composition of the tertiary sector in these economies A review of the definitions of the services sector shows that the scope of this sector is getting widened. It encompasses in addition to conventional services, many new services also. The services boom that we have been currently experiencing in our country has played a very important role in changing the traditional perception of the country from a 'land of beggars' , 'snake charmers' and 'cyber–coolies' of yesteryears to a 'land of knowledge workers' and making India noticeable globally. She also points towards the flip side of the growth of IIT and ITES segment.

Dr Joshi tries to identify the variables, which influence the tertiary sector employment. Based on a sample of twenty-four developing countries she finds that human development index is an important determinant of the percentage of labour force engaged in the tertiary sector. Other factors include urbanisation, work force participation rate and percentage of labour force engaged in the manufacturing sector.

She also addresses the question of sustainability of a high economic growth driven by the isolated growth of the services sector in the long run. She holds the view that the services sector which will continue to enable the country to attain a 8 per cent plus GDP growth rate will, through inter-sectoral linkages, generate momentum for creation of employment opportunities and poverty reduction.

Undoubtedly, increasing affluence, changing consumption patterns, increasing demand for life style products, increasing urbanisation, growing middle class and "burgeoning youth brigade" (demographic dividend) have acted as a buffer for services growth in India. However, within the services sector, there are a wide array of unconventional services *viz.* professional services, IT and ITES, telecom services, organised retail, eco-tourism, health tourism etc. which are the main drivers of services sector growth, though conventional services like unorganised retail, real estate and entertainment services too are contributing to services growth.

In view of the ongoing 'service revolution' in our economy and the vast export growth potential of commercial services and the provision of the multi-lateral framework for international trade in services under GATS, further liberalisation of trade in services is pertinent at the present juncture. She while pointing towards the growth potential of health services cautions on the one hand that liberalisation of trade in services should be accompanied by safeguard measures and emphasises on the introduction of more reforms in agriculture and manufacturing sectors on the other, as isolated growth of services is not desirable for the long-term growth and its sustainability.

This is an important study which provides a wealth of information about the tertiary sector by dealing with questions ranging from concept to composition of services, from excessiveness to adequacy of services growth, from determinants of service sector employment to drivers of services sector growth and from sustainability of isolated growth of services to significance of trade in services.

Arup Mitra
(*Professor of Economics*)
Institute of Economic Growth,
Delhi

Acknowledgements

I am deeply indebted and grateful to Professor Arup Mitra, Institute of Economic Growth, New Delhi for his generous help, continuous support and constructive suggestions which have greatly helped me in improving my research work and contributed towards creating the present work.

I would like to express my sincere gratitude, warm and most cordial thanks to Professor L.R. Sharma. Without his invaluable directions, incessant impetus and healthy criticism it would have been difficult for me to accomplish the present work.

I am extremely grateful to Professor V.N. Pandit, Sri Sathya Sai Institute of Higher Learning, Prasanthi Nilayam., Professor Ramesh Chand, National Professor, National Centre for Agricultural Economics and Policy Research, Dr. Bhim Sen Singh, Principal, Kirori Mal College, Prof. D.B. Gupta, Chairman, Governing Body, Kirori Mal College and Dr. P.L. Sanjeeva Reddy, Director (Retd.), Indian Institute of Public Administration for their encouragement.

I express endless thanks to my husband, Sandeep Joshi and to my loving, caring and understanding children Saumya and Ananay who have been perennial source of inspiration to me in furthering the cause of my academic pursuits.

I offer my thanks and deep gratitude for my revered parents who have always been a source of inspiration for me. It is with their love, blessings, material and moral support that I have been able to complete this work. At this point I feel a bit sad about my father, who having been a strong motivational force does not understand the relevance of current work after loss of memory in a serious accident. His encouraging words still echo in my ears and will continue driving me to take many such challenging assignments in future.

To each of the persons directly and indirectly involved in completion of this book my sincere thanks once again.

1

Tertiary Sector in Developing Economies

Growth and Structure

Introduction

These days economic development is being defined in terms of structural change. That is the reason why the study of structural change is important. "Structural change permits viable growth to occur, and growth provides the material for subsequent structural change" (Uphoff and Ilchman, 1972). According to structuralists (Fisher, 1935; Clark, 1960; Kuznets, 1966, 1969, 1972; Chenery and Syrquin, 1970), as the process of economic development proceeds, the share of agricultural sector in national income and employment—which is typically high in the early stages of development—begins to decline and that of non-agricultural sectors experience a rise. This has become almost a universal phenomenon and holds true in case of all the countries which experienced or are experiencing economic development. The relatively faster growth of tertiary sector *vis-à-vis* other broad sectors of the economies (which emerges from our analysis) has given rise to contemporary issues which require much debate. The topicality of our discussion in this book arises in this context.

Numerous studies have been devoted to the growth of the agricultural and manufacturing sectors of the developing countries, but the services sector has received far too inadequate attention from the researchers. Even Colin Clark rued this fact as far back as 1940, when he said that, "the economics of tertiary industry remains to be written." In 1968, V.R. Fuchs pointed out that the services sector has "long been the stepchild of economic research."[1] Cowell (1984: 3) quotes Lewis as

1. Gershuny and Miles, 1983: 10

saying that "contemporary economic theories and statistics are biased in their treatment of services and emphasise that these should be legitimised as valid forms of wealth and the myth regarding their non-productive character should be dispelled" (Cowell, 1984: 3).

In this connection, Bhalla (1970: 519) has rightly noted that "with the exception of a few recent empirical studies, economic literature has continued to neglect the growing services sector of the less developed countries. While writers like Kuznets, Stigler and Fuchs, it is true, have done a great deal to meet Colin Clark's complaint that 'the eonomics of tertiary industry remains to be written' most work in this field has focused on the economy of the United States or the advanced countries of Western Europe." Keeping in view the hypothesis that emerges from this study, *viz.*, that the services have been either growing at a faster rate than the primary and secondary sectors in several developing economies or growing quite rapidly in most developing economies, there seems to be a serious research gap in this respect.

Further, the treatment of this sector as 'residual sector' and the association of services with 'luxuries', 'inessentials' and with the satisfaction of psychological and emotional needs rather than physical needs; with 'invisible items' in the balance of payments (BoP), etc., are clear-cut manifestations of the discriminatory treatment meted out to them (Cowell, 1984). Therefore, there is a need for the recognition of the actual and potential role of this sector.

The importance of the tertiary sector lies in the fact, as pointed out by W.A. Lewis, that the income elasticity of demand for services is the highest among the three broad sectors (agriculture, industry and services). To quote him, "The income elasticity of demand for manufactures exceed unity, and the income elasticity for food is less than unity. The income elasticity of demand for services is higher even than for manufactures (Lewis, 1955: 278). It is thus ironical that such an important component of the developing economies has remained by and large unresearched.

The Uruguay Round of the General Agreement on Tariffs and Trade (GATT) had in fact thrown the services sector onto the centre stage of international negotiations. Such a sector, therefore, needs to be studied more thoroughly than has been the case so far.

The present chapter focuses on growth and structure of the tertiary sector in developing economies. Chapter 2 attempts to analyse nature and relative growth of the tertiary sector in developing economies. The main focal points of Chapter 3 are composition of tertiary sector and inter-temporal changes therein. It also highlights in brief the emergence and role of new services in the Indian economy. The question of 'excess and 'adequate' growth of the services sector has been examined in Chapter 4. In Chapter 5 an attempt has been made to empirically verify the determinants of tertiary sector employment in developing economies. Chapter 6 highlights the crucial role that can be played by the tertiary sector in employment generation and poverty alleviation and also on complementarity of the growth of commodity producing and tertiary sectors. Chapter 7 points towards the boom in services sector of India and main drivers of service sector growth. The last chapter focuses on GATS, Indian services sector and trade potential in health services.

Sectoral Composition of Production and Employment in Developing Economies

It is by now a well established fact that the per capita income is negatively correlated to the share of agricultural output and employment, and positively correlated to the share of non-agricultural output in GNP and employment (Clark, 1960; Kuznets, 1966; Chenery and Syrquin, 1977; Kindleberger, 1977). It would be of interest to consider the empirical evidence in this regard. A. Holub has suggested a method of demonstrating these associations as below:

> If agriculture, industry and services are denoted by the letters, 'A', 'I' and 'S' respectively and if these sectors are ranked in order of their proportion in total production and employment, the traditional, transitional and modern production and employment structures may be expressed as ASI & AIS, IAS & ISA and SAI & SIA respectively. In all, six types of sectoral structures can be distinguished—ASI, AIS, IAS, ISA, SIA and SAI.

These patterns were viewed as historical stages in the development of sectoral structures by A. Holub.

Taking a sample of 59 developing countries for which complete data relating to the share of agriculture, industry and services in the overall

GDP are available in the *World Development Report*, 1992 and 2007, we have used the foregoing Holub's methodology to characterise the sectoral structures of the sample countries. The relevant figures are given in Table 1.1.

It is evident from Table 1.1 that in 1965, the traditional, transitional and modern structures, according to Holub's typology existed in 37 per cent, 3.7 per cent and 59.3 per cent countries respectively. But the whole scenario changed by the year 2005. In that year the percentage of countries characterised by the traditional structure of production declined to 15.3 per cent while the countries which attained the characteristics of modern structure registered a sharp rise from 59.3 per cent to 72.8 per cent.

Table 1.1

Typology of Production Structure in Developing Countries, 1965-2005

Type of Production Structure	*Number of Countries*	
	1965	*2005*
(i) Traditional (ASI & AIS)	20 (37)	9 (15.3)
(ii) Transitional (IAS & ISA)	2 (3.7)	7 (11.9)
(iii) Modern (SAI & SIA)	32 (59.3)	43 (72.8)

Note: 1. The symbols used for denoting the traditional, transitional and modern structures of production are:

Structural Type	Share in GDP
ASI	Agriculture>Services>Industry
AIS	Agriculture>Industry>Services
IAS	Industry>Agriculture>Services
ISA	Industry>Services>Agriculture
SAI	Services>Agriculture>Industry
SIA	Services>Industry>Agriculture

2. Figures in parentheses show the percentage of total countries in the sample.
3. The percentages of countries are calculated by excluding from the sample five countries in 1965, the structure of production of which does not tally with the above mentioned three production structures.

Source: Calculated from figures in World Bank, *World Development Report*, Various Issues.

Table 1.2

Structural Typology in Terms of Employment, 1965-2000

Type of Production Structure		Number of Countries	
		1965	2000
(i)	Traditional (ASI & AIS)	23 (74.2)	8 (25.8)
(ii)	Transitional (IAS & ISA)	1 (3.2)	-
(iii)	Modern (SAI & SIA)	7 (22.6)	23 (74.2)

Note: 1. Figures in parentheses show the percentage of total countries in the sample.
2. Due to non-availability of data for the year 2000, in case of some countries we have taken 1998 or 1999 as the current year.

Sources: 1. Calculated from figures in World Bank, *World Development Report*, 1985.
2. ILO, *Yearbook of Labour Statistics*, 2001.

By applying the Holub's strategy to employment structures of a sample of 31 developing countries for which complete data relating to the share of the three sectors of these economies in total employment are available in the *World Development Report, 1985* and ILO, *Year Book of Labour Statistics 2001*, we observe from Table 1.2 that in 1965, traditional structure of employment, dominated by agricultural share existed in as many as 74.2 per cent countries in this sample. In sharp contrast to it, the transitional and modern structures of employment were seen only in 3.2 per cent and 22.6 per cent countries respectively. In 2000, the number of countries where the traditional structure persisted declined to 25.8 per cent while the countries with modern structure of employment rose to 74.2 per cent. Thus, we notice that there has been taking place a growing 'tertiarisation' of the structures of production and employment in many developing countries.

Relative Sectoral Labour Productivity

The question of relative sectoral labour productivities (defined as the ratio between the proportion of GDP originating in a sector and the proportion of labour force employed in that sector) has been taken up in this section keeping in view the fact that the process of structural transition which we have analysed above is initially spurred by a disequilibrium in the factor markets and the disequilibrium gets progressively corrected as the transition is completed.

Chenery and Syrquin (1977: 53) provide a striking illustration of this disequilibrium. Their hypothesis in this connection is that at a low level of income per capita, relative labour productivity in the primary sector declines from 70 per cent to 50 per cent. But as the income level rises, labour productivity differential between primary production on the one hand and industry and services on the other gets reduced quite substantially due to migration of labour force from the former to the latter, thereby correcting the structural disequilibrium.

Clark (1940: 318) in this context states that, "in countries which have a markedly low productivity in primary and secondary industry, tertiary industries have a productivity much above the national average, and this indeed accounts for the rapid transfer of population into tertiary employment."

It seems that the relative labour productivity differential referred to above is responsible in these countries for a change in the pattern of employment, with labour shifting out of the low productivity primary sector and into the secondary and tertiary sectors as observed by us earlier. But as the productivity differential narrows down, the intersectoral migration of labour slows down.

In this connection, we took a sample of 61 developing countries and calculated relative labour productivities for the three sectors. For the economy as a whole the relative labour productivity index is one; indices of sector higher than one indicates higher labour productivity than in the economy as a whole.

We observed that the agricultural labour productivity index was less than that of the economy as a whole in 93.4 per cent countries in 1965 as well as in 1981. This can be attributed to the larger share of agriculture in total labour force (because of it being the residual labour employing sector) than in GDP. The relative labour productivity rates of industrial and tertiary sectors were greater than that of the economy as a whole in 95.1 per cent and 90.2 per cent countries respectively in 1965 as well as 1981.

As between the three sectors, we noticed that in 1965, the relative labour productivity in the services sectors was the highest in 65.6 per cent countries. In 1981, the number of countries where the relative labour productivity rate in the services sector was the highest, however, declined to 54.1 per cent.

It is our hunch that by the 1960s, labour absorption in agriculture merely on account of spillover of labour force to this residual sector, had reached a saturation point and the abysmally low labour productivity in agriculture had thus resulted. The much higher labour productivity in the secondary and especially tertiary sectors had started attracting such surplus labour, and in combination with other demand factors, had resulted in a relatively high growth rate of the non-agricultural sectors, especially the tertiary sector. But a high growth rate of this sector in recent years, as observed earlier, has started pushing down labour productivity in the tertiary sector in subsequent years, which perhaps accounts for a relatively small number of countries registering highest relative labour productivity in 1981.

Conclusions

The following features of growth and structure of tertiary sector in the developing economies over the period 1965-2000/2005 emerge from the foregoing analysis:

(a) We observed that in 1965, 37 per cent countries were characterised by the traditional structure of production. But in 2005 their number declined significantly and more than half of the developing economies attained the modern structure of production.

(b) In terms of employment the traditional structure continued to persist in 25.8 per cent of developing economies, 74.2 per cent countries attained the modern structure, in the year 2000.

(c) It seems that the relative labour productivity differential has been substantially responsible for the observed process of structural change, especially in favour of the tertiary sector in the 1960s and the 1970s. But as the productivity differential has narrowed down, the growth potential of the tertiary sector, especially in the middle-income economies has come to be exhausted.

References

Bhalla, A.S. (1970). "The Role of Services in Employment Expansion", *International Labour Review*, Vol. 101, Jan-June.

Chenery, H.B. and Moises Syrquin (1977). *Patterns of Development, 1950-70*. Oxford: Oxford University Press.

Clark, Colin (1940). *The Conditions of Economic Progress*. Second Edition. Macmillian and Co. Ltd.

———. (1960). *Condition of Economic Progress*, Third Edition. London: Macmillan.

Cowell, D.W. (1984). *The Marketing of Services*. London: Heinemann.

ESCAP and UNIDO (1982). "Industrialisation Trends in the Developing ESCAP Region", *Economic Bulletin for Asia and the Pacific*, December.

Fisher, A.G.B. (1935). "Economic Implications of Material Progress", *International Labour Review*, July.

———. (1939). "Primary, Secondary and Tertairy Production", *Economic Record*, June.

Gershuny, Jonathan. I. and I.D. Miles (1983). *The New Service Economy: The Transformation of Employment in Industrial Societies*. London: Frances Printer Publishers.

Holub, A. (1970). "A Brief Review of Structural Development in the Developing ECAFE Countries", *Economic Bulletin for Asia and the Far East*, July/September.

Kindleberger, C.P. and Bruce Herrick (1977). *Economic Development*, 3rd Edition. Tokyo: McGraw Hill, Kogakusha Ltd.

Kuznets, Simon (1966). *Economic Growth and Structure, Selected Essays*. London: Heinemann, Educational Books.

———. (1966). *Modern Economic Growth*. Calcutta: Oxford and IBH Publishing Co.

———. (1969). *Economic Growth and Structure*, Selected Essays. Calcutta: Oxford and IBH Publishing Co.

———. (1972). *Economic Growth of Nations, Total Output and Production Structure*. Cambridge: Harvard University Press.

Lewis, W.A. (1955). *The Theory of Economic Growth*. London: Novello and Company Ltd.

Uphoff, Norman. T. and Warren F. Ilchman (1972). *The Political Economy of Development*. Berkeley: University of California Press.

This chapter is a modified version of an article titled "Tertiary Sector in Developing Economies: Growth and Structure", *Economic Analyst*, XIII(1&2): 9-18. 1992.

2

Tertiary Sector in Developing Economies

Its Nature and Relative Growth

Introduction

Economic development has been defined in terms of structural change, but the nature of structural change in question has varied from time to time. The contemporary meaning of development is in terms of a structural change in the redistribution and utilisation of the GNP, for some in favour of the poorer sections of society, and for others in favour of building people's capabilities, or promoting human development. This is of course, a normative concept of development, which lays down norms for redistribution of GNP so that structurally it would result in benefits to the poorer sections of society. The older economists, being concerned with positive changes rather than normative ones, empirically studied changes in the origin of GNP from the three broad sectors. In the present chapter an attempt has been made to deal with this latter form of structural change. It attempts to analyse in this context the growth of tertiary sector *vis-à-vis* the material production sectors in developing economies in general and in India in particular.

Historical Development of the Use of the Concept of 'Tertiary Sector'[1]

There is no consensus on the definition of tertiary sector. To understand fully as to why ambiguity still prevails concerning the concept of tertiary sector, we shall first of all examine the historical development of the use of the term 'services' here. The physiocratic

1. This section is based on Cowell, 1984: 19-21.

school of thought consisting of a group of French philosophers of 18th century is generally considered to mark the beginning of economics as a systematic field of study. According to this school of thought, agriculture alone was productive because it yielded net income and all other non-agricultural occupations were 'sterile' as they just recouped the cost incurred on them.

Adam Smith criticised the physiocrats for describing manufacturing, trade and transportation as altogether barren and non-productive occupations and he himself included most of them in the category of productive labour. He stated that these other branches of 'material goods production' were just as capable of returning a net income to producers as was agriculture. He drew a line of distinction between productive and unproductive labour. According to him, productiveness depended upon 'tangibility' which in turn was associated with the durability of the economic activity. But applying his criterion of tangibility and durability he concluded that services because of their intangible and, therefore, non-durable nature were "barren and unproductive because they perish generally in the very instant of their performance and do not fix or realise themselves in any vendible commodity."[2] We will discuss Smithian and Marxian perspective on productive and unproductive labour more fully in the following section.

Jean Baptiste Say, in contrast, defined productive activities as those "which have/enjoy utility and give satisfaction to the consumers." Alfred Marshall carried this concept further and observed that, "men cannot create matter." What a man can do in the physical world is that with his efforts and sacrifices he can only add to the utility of a matter either by changing its form or its arrangement, just as, for example, table can be made from a log of wood.

He argued that, "there was no scientific foundation for making a distinction between the activities of the cabinet maker and the furniture dealer, the railway carrying coal above ground and the miner carrying it underground, the fisherman and fishmonger; all produce utilities. In other words, all activities are providing services to satisfy wants."[3]

---

2. ibid.: 20.
3. ibid.

The divide or gap between goods and services has been further bridged by more recent views which suggest that the only point of distinction between a good and service is that a service does not lead to a change in the form of a good.

Table 2.1 given below sets out a summary of these different views on services.

Table 2.1

Historical Definitions of Service

The Physiocrats (c. 1750)	All activities other than agricultural production
Adam Smith (1723-1790)	All activities that do not end in tangible products
J.B. Say (1767-1832)	All non-manufacturing activities that add utility to goods
Alfred Marshall (1842-1924)	Goods (services) that pass out of existence at the moment of creation
Western Countries (1925-1960)	Services do not lead to a change in the form of a good
Contemporary	An activity that does not lead to a change in the form of a good

Source: Walters and Bergiel, 1982: 483.

From the foregoing, it appears that too much emphasis was laid by early economists on the importance of primary and secondary sectors and Adam Smith's misinterpretation of service activities as barren, parasitic and non-productive not only resulted in the neglect of analysis of this sector but also acted as hindrance in the development of a precise and unanimously accepted definition of tertiary sector.

Productive and Unproductive Labour: Smithian and Marxian Perspectives

Since the present analysis deals with the distinction between services and material production, it may be useful here to consider the Smithian and Marxian distinction between productive and unproductive labour. According to the dichotomy between the material producing and service producing sectors of the economy, all the agricultural and manufacturing activities are clubbed under 'material producing sector' while the services sector is generally considered to be the residual sector of the economy consisting of activities other than producing goods. To call 'tertiary sector' as 'residual sector' will be a misnomer if the vital role which this sector has been playing in the developed and underdeveloped economies of the world is taken into account. One of the reasons for its being treated as residual sector is Smith's misinterpretation of service activities and in it he was later on supported by Karl Marx. Whatever may be the reasons responsible for less favourable treatment which is meted out to this sector the fact is, as Tucker (1977: 13) says "this distinction (between goods and services producing sectors) has identifiable historical precedent. It continues to carry with it the misleading parallel dichotomy of 'productive' and 'unproductive labour'." In this context, we shall briefly examine the Smithian and Marxian perspectives on productive and unproductive labour in this sub-section, and in the next one we shall focus on the imprint which their views have left on the national accounting systems as being used currently.

Over two hundred years ago Adam Smith distinguished between productive and unproductive labour and described services as ephemeral, non-durable and non-productive because he believed that their production and consumption slows down the process of capital accumulation, economic growth and development.

Smith (1910: 145-46) distinguished between productive and unproductive labour and observes in this context that, "there is one sort of labour which adds to the value of the subject upon which it is bestowed; there is another which has no such effect. The former, as it produces a value may be called productive: the latter, unproductive labour."

He further elaborated on the nature of 'unproductive labour' by arguing that, "the labour of a menial servant...adds to the value of nothing...The labour of some of the most respectable orders in the society is, like that of menial servants, unproductive of any value, and does not fix or realise itself in any permanent subject, or vendible commodity, which endures after that labour is past...Their services how honourable, how useful, or how necessary so ever produces nothing for which an equal quantity of service can afterwards be procured...In the same class must be ranked...Churchmen, lawyers, physicians, men of letters of all kinds, players, buffoons, musicians, opera singers, opera dancers, etc." (ibid).

Thus, from the above quotation it is clear that, in Smith's opinion, unproductive labour was that labour which (a) was unproductive of any value, (b) unproductive of surplus value, and (c) does not result in any permanent subject or saleable commodity.

In the category of productive labour, he included those engaged in agriculture, manufacturing, commerce (trade) and the transportation of goods, but on the other hand, classified the sovereign, all the civil and military personnel of government, the professions, those engaged in the performance of personal services, domestic services and services of dwellings to be unproductive labour.[4]

Unlike William Petty and Boisguilibert (the proponents of 'comprehensive production concept', who defined national income in comprehensive terms as embracing both goods and services), Smith included in his concept of national product only saleable material goods and services like commerce and transportation.

In the last quarter of the 19th century, two important theoretical developments took place. One involved the criticism of Smithian viewpoints and a return to the 'comprehensive production concept' of the 17th century, and the other involved the revival, reformulation and extension of Smith's original 'Restricted Material Production concept' by Karl Marx.

Revival of Smithian Material Production Concept by Karl Marx

At the time, when Smith's Restricted Material Production concept was about to be discarded, it received powerful support from Karl Marx. He offered a new version of Smith's concept in his posthumously published books, *Das Capital* (Vol. II, 1885) and *Theories of Surplus Value* (1904).[5]

Like Smith, Marx (1909: 971 & 979) too included agriculture, mining and manufacturing in the category of material production. But he was

4. This and the following two paragraphs are based on Studenski, 1958: 12 & 19.

5. ibid.: 21.

not as positive as Smith was about the inclusion of trade in this category. He excluded government services from the field of production as Smith did. However, the reasons advanced by them are somewhat different. Marx excluded them not only on the grounds that government services are not marketable or they are not governed by the principles of capitalistic production generally, but because he questions their utility also. He considered government as an agent of the exploiting class which helps them to oppress the workers.[6]

Marx included the transportation of goods in the material production category but he was not clear as to whether transportation of passengers is a part of material production or immaterial production. This point becomes amply clear when on the one hand he remarks that, "in addition to mining, agriculture and heavy industry, there exists fourth sphere of material production... This industry is transportation, whether of men or goods. The relationship of the productive or wage workers to the capitalists is absolutely the same in this as in other spheres of material production" (Marx, 1952: 328).

But in succeeding line he says that "the transportation of mankind one might say, is simply a service rendered by an entrepreneur," (ibid.) thus indicating it to be a part of immaterial production.

Marx ofcourse admired Smith for being the first one to introduce the proposition that under capitalistic system that labour is productive which produces profit and capital for the entrepreneur, but he also criticised him for not sticking to this definition more consistently and for not drawing all the relevant conclusions from it.[7]

National Accounting Systems in the Present Century

In the preceding and the present century, the division of support between the two major production concepts, *viz.*, the comprehensive concept and the limited material production concept, has come to be drawn along political ideologies followed in different countries.

All the countries which have been outside the erstwhile Soviet bloc base their national income estimates on the comprehensive production

6. Studenski, 1958: 184.

7. ibid.: 22.

concept which is broader and has more rational foundation. This concept has achieved the status of international standard with the organisation and entry of United Nations Organization into the field of national income accounting after the World War II.

In contrast to it, all the socialist countries where Marxian doctrine was or has been in vogue subscribed to the material production concept of national income as revised by Marx.[8]

The socialist countries included in the corpus of material production all "those activities which create material goods or help in production processes, *viz.*, gathering, extracting or growing raw materials, processing the latter into finished products, and delivering them to the intermediate or final uses" (Wilczynki, 1970: 60).

According to the official socialist classification (ibid.: 60-61), the broad material production is made up of the following six major divisions which have been arranged in the descending order of importance attached to each of them. These are:

i) Industry.

ii) Construction.

iii) Agriculture.

iv) Transport.

v) Trade.

vi) Other Material Production.

The remaining forms of activities are included in unproductive class and, therefore, these are excluded from national income estimates. These are usually classified under eight groupings:

i) Public Administration and Justice.

ii) Education Science and Culture.

iii) Health, Social Welfare and Sport.

iv) Finance and Insurance.

v) Local Government and Housing Administration.

8. ibid.: 24.

vi) Defence.

vii) Political, Social and Religious Activities.

viii) Other Services.

Thus, it can be concluded from the preceding discussion that in comparison with the non-socialist countries, the system of national income accounts in socialist countries was based on Smithian Restricted Material Production concept as revised by Marx which is a somewhat narrower concept of production.

This is an indicator of the deep imprint that Smithian and Marxian views on productive and unproductive labour had left on the national accounting system of socialist countries.

On the other hand, the concept of national income accounting developed by the UNO and other multilateral financial institutions, which is commonly in use in most countries of the world, uses a comprehensive measure of national income, encompassing both the material production sectors and the services sectors.

Production and Employment in the Material *vis-à-vis* Services Production Sectors

Here, we shall briefly discuss the composition of GDP and employment of developing countries at a slightly more aggregate level *viz.*, the material *vis-à-vis* services production sectors at two points of time, *viz.*, 1965 and 2005. The change in composition of national output takes place on account of different rates of growth of these two broad sectors. The share of the one whose growth rate is faster will rise while that of slow growing sector will decline. These changes in the relative growth rates of the two, as reflected in the composition of GDP at two different points of time are shown in Table 2.2.

In this Table we have taken a sample of 59 countries for studying relative growth of the broad material production and services sectors as reflected in changes in the structure of production of these developing countries between the years 1965 and 2005.

Table 2.2

Change in Sectoral Composition of GDP between 1965 and 2005

Changes in Percentage Share to GDP	*Material Production Sectors Number of Countries*	*Services Sector Number of Countries*
Increase	13 (22.03)	44 (74.6)
Decrease	45 (76.3)	15 (25.4)
Constant	01 (1.7)	—

Note: 1. Material production sectors comprise primary and secondary sectors.
2. The figures in the parentheses are percentages.

Source: Computed by us from figures in the World Bank, *World Development Report*,1992 Table 3, pp.222-23 and *World Development Report*, 2007, Table 4, pp.294-95.

At a glance, it is clear from the figures provided in the Table that during the period 1965-2005, the share of the material production sectors in total output shrank in as many as 76.3 per cent countries of the sample. It is clear that as material production sectors witnessed a decline in their share in GDP in these countries, the services sector recorded a corresponding increase in its share in 74.6 per cent countries. However, these figures in the Table also show perverse changes in that the share of material production sectors in GDP increased in 22.03 per cent countries and remained constant in 1.7 per cent countries. One possible reason for this perverse change is that the material production sector comprises primary and secondary sectors. So even when the GDP originating from primary sector declines, the share of GDP originating from secondary sector may be increasing thereby, increasing the share of material production sector in overall GDP.

Thus, from the above it is clear that the services sector has grown faster in majority of the countries.

In order to observe disparate growth rates of services *vis-à-vis* material production sectors, Table 2.3 focuses on the changes which occurred in the composition of employment between 1975 and 2001.

We can see from Table 2.3 that over the 1975-2001 period the share of the broad material production sector declined in all the sample countries except two, i.e., Nicaragua and Uruguay. A contrast to this picture can be noticed in case of the services sector. The share of this sector in overall employment increased in all countries with the exception of three countries *viz.*, Botswana, Nicaragua and Uruguay. This share varied between as low as 19.6 per cent in Sri Lanka to as high as 64.8 per cent in Puerto Rico in 1975, and between as low as 35.3 per cent in Sri Lanka in 2001 to 80.3 per cent in Hongkong in the same year.

Table 2.3

Composition of Employment in Material Production vis-à-vis Services Production Sectors, 1975-2001

(Proportion of Total Employment in Percentage)

	Country	Year	Material Production Sectors	Services Production Sector
1.	Bolivia	1975	66.6	33.4
		2000	23.1	42.6
2.	Botswana	1975	38.9	61.1
		2001	37.8	53.6
3.	Brasil	1975	55.7	42.1
		2001	40.6	59.4
4.	Chile	1975	46.7	52.6
		2001	23.9	62.5
5.	Costa Rica	1976	57.5	42.0
		2001	38.9	60.5
6.	Egypt	1975	66.7	32.1
		2001	49.8	49.9
7.	Honduras	1975	76.5	23.5
		2001	62.3	35.1
8.	Hongkong	1976	53.3	41.0
		2001	19.7	80.3
9.	Israel	1975	40.2	59.3
		2001	38.5	72.3
10.	Korea, Rep. of	1975	69.6	30.4
		2001	37.4	61.5
11.	Nicaragua	1975	49.7	63.0
		2001	58.1	38.2
12.	Pakistan	1975	73.3	26.4
		2001	66.5	33.5
13.	Panama	1975	48.9	46.9
		2001	35.4	58.9

contd. ...

...contd. ... *(Proportion of Total Employment in Percentage)*

Country	Year	Material Production Sectors	Services Production Sector
14. Puerto Rico	1975	35.5	64.8
	2001	15.5	76.4
15. Sri Lanka	1975	81.1	19.6
	2002	59.0	35.3
16. Turkey	1975	77.0	21.8
	2001	60.3	39.0
17. Uruguay	1976	35.3	64.5
	2001	50.4	62.8
18. Venezuela	1975	45.0	54.9
	2001	31.7	68.2

Note: 1. Material Production sector comprises agriculture, hunting, forestry, fishing, mining and quarrying, manufacturing, electricity, gas, water supply and construction activities. In the services sector we have clubbed together wholesale and retail trade, restaurants, hotels, transport, storage, communication, finance, insurance, real estate and business services and also community, social and personal services.

2. In case of some countries the figures do not add up to 100 as data on some components of two broad sectors was not available.

Source: International Labour Office, *Yearbook of Labour Statistics* (Various Issues).

Looking at these long term changes observed in the composition of GDP and employment due to the slower growth of the broad material production sector and faster growth of the services sector, it is noted that a process of structural shifts, in favour of the tertiary sector, is underway in most developing countries of the world.

Basic Explanations for the Relative Growth of the Services Sector

It may be deduced from the foregoing that during the course of economic development, the service sector grows quite rapidly (both in terms of its contribution to GNP and employment) relative to the other two sectors *viz.*, agricultural and industrial sectors. In other words, there takes place a growing 'Tertiarisation'[9] of the structures of production and employment. Consequently, the tertiary sector becomes quite prominent because the primary sector loses its primacy and the manufacturing sector gets relegated to secondary position. Now the

9. This term has been used by Marshall, 1988: 4.

question arises: What is the rationale behind the process? Several basic reasons which have been advanced for the relative growth of the service sector are enumerated below.

Virtually all of the writers on the subject, including Fisher, Clark, Ojala, Kuznets, Campbell, Arthur Lewis, etc., have stressed the role of changes in the composition of demand with rising per capita income.[10] They particularly emphasise the sectoral differences in income elasticity of demand. Since income elasticity of demand for services is observed to be more than unity and even higher than for manufactured goods, the demand for services tends to rise more rapidly as higher levels of income are attained. This in turn leads to the proliferation of this particular sector.

Victor. R. Fuchs has put forward three explanations for the drastic shift of employment in favour of services. These are:

i) Slow growth of labour productivity in services as compared to the other sectors of the economy.

ii) The growth in intermediate demand for services of firms producing goods.

iii) The growth in final demand for services from consumers.

Fuchs (1968: 3-5), in his study relating to United States, found the lower output per man in services sector to be the major cause of the shift of employment towards services sector. He suggested the following reasons why this was so:

a) There was a greater decline in hours worked per man in services than in industry.

b) The quality of labour increased more rapidly in industry than in service.

c) There was a difference in the physical capital per worker available in industry compared with services.

d) The technological progress was more rapid in industry than in service and the former also benefited more from growing economies of scale.

---

10. Johnston, 1971: 373.

Some weaknesses in these suggestions as pointed out by Cowell (1984: 12), are that it is difficult to measure output changes in services. Further, non-availability of adequate statistics make it difficult to describe accurately comparative changes in the various sectors of the economy.

Fuchs attributes a part of the explanation for the growth of services to the growth of intermediate demand for services (like banking, insurance, transport, accounting and consultancy services, etc.) which occur with the growth of an economy.

The third explanation put forward in this context is the growth of final demand from consumers. This explanation is based on the assumption that there are differences between income and spending patterns of goods and services. It is argued that with the increase in income, consumer spending on services like travel, education, recreation, health care and similar other services increases more than proportionately.

Fuchs, however, opines that it is difficult to measure the relationship between income and demand for various outputs i.e. income elasticity of demand for services relative to other outputs. This is so because for calculating elasticities, measures of real output or consumption are required. However, for many services and some other industries accurate measures of real output are not available. Moreover, demand depends upon many variables *viz.*, changes in relative prices, tastes, technology, urbanisation and the distribution of income. Besides, there may be time lag involved in the adjustment of spending pattern to changes in income; then the pattern observed at any given moment may depend upon current as well as past levels of income. Finally, elasticities change from time to time.[11]

Besides, there are other factors too which lead to the growth of final demand of the consumers. These are: changed life styles, more leisure time, longer life expectancy, increasing complexity of life, increasing affluence and technological developments, etc.[12]

Table 2.4 gives a summary of reasons for the growth of consumer services as advanced by W.F. Schoell and J.T. Ivy.

11. Fuchs, 1968: 41 and also see Fuchs, 1965: 351-352.

12. Cowell, 1984: 13.

Table 2.4

Reasons for the Growth of Demand for Services Industries

1. Increasing affluence	Greater demand for lawn care, carpet cleaning, car cleaning and other services that consumers used to provide for themselves
2. More leisure	Greater demand for travel agencies, travel resorts, adult education courses
3. High percentage of women in the labour force	Greater demand for day care nurseries, maid services, away-from-home meals
4. Greater life expectancy	Greater demand for nursing homes and health care services
5. Greater complexity of products	Greater demand for skilled specialists to provide maintenance for such complex products as cars and home computers
6. Increasing complexity of life	Greater demand for income tax preparers, marriage counsellors, legal advisers, employment services
7. Greater concern about ecology and resource scarcity	Greater demand for purchased or leased services, such as door-to-door bus service and car rental instead of car ownership
8. Increasing number of new products	The computer–sparked development of such service as programming, repair and time sharing

Source: Schoell and Ivy, 1981: 277.

Besides per capita income, there are, however, other factors also which affect economic structure in various ways. These factors are not necessarily connected with the level of development and even when they are connected, they may not be reflected in the income level. This point is made by G.J. Stigler, who argues that per capita national income represents the principal factor influencing industrial structure (especially as regards services), but that the correspondence is never uniform or complete. Stigler lists several other factors which directly affect the share of services in the GNP: the processes of urbanisation and specialisation, technological change, rising educational standards, a trend towards greater equality of income distribution, and increase in the average age of population which is a consequence of fall in birth rates and improvement in medical care.[13] In addition to it, Galenson (1963) holds the view point that the expansion of manufacturing activity pushes up the consumption of services and also creates induced demand for various service inputs.

13. Ofer, 1967: 16-17.

As against the above-mentioned hypothesis relying on demand factors, Kuznets (1966: 104) has particularly laid stress on "the importance of changes in the production or supply side in explaining changes in the industrial distribution of total product among the major and minor sectors...." He suggests that the very processes of industrialisation and urbanisation have brought about changes on the supply side. Data presented by him relating to US and Sweden show a very sharp decline in the percentage of income devoted to food and a considerable increase in the proportion of income spent on processing, transportation and distribution of food products.

He attributes the growth of these three services to various technical innovations and other factors that influence consumer preferences. He identifies two factors that have had a significant impact in altering the composition of final demand. These are: innovations that have changed the character of goods and services to consumers and changes in relative prices associated with differential changes in productivity.

Thus, from the above it is clear that there are primarily two factors, namely 'supply push' and 'demand induced' factors which account for structural shifts in favour of tertiary sector resulting in substantial growth of employment in tertiary activities.

However, the above-mentioned factors do not exhaust the explanations given in this respect and there are further hypotheses which have been given by different writers for the growth of services sector employment in developing countries. These are given below.

Demographic Factors

There are two demographic factors which are generally cited for the growth of employment of the tertiary sector in developing countries, *viz.* population pressure and rural-urban migration. These two factors are interlinked. Population has been increasing quite rapidly in many developing countries. In many of these countries, the problem has assumed the form of 'population explosion'.[14] But the agricultural sector alone is unable to absorb the consequently growing labour force. So initially there takes place a shift of active workers towards secondary

---

14. World Bank, 1993: 288-289, Table 26.

and finally towards tertiary sectors. Since tertiary activities are mainly urban activities, therefore, migration of population from rural to urban areas takes place. Migration is itself the spillover effect of growing population. In other words, the process of urbanisation gathers momentum.[15] This is accompanied by growth of mainly urban informal sector tertiary employment which is mainly labour-intensive. However, Sabolo (1975: 143-45) termed this as a 'superficial explanation' which claims the growth of employment in service industries of developing countries to be essentially of 'residual character'. He says that this explanation is true only in case of traditional activities like street vending and domestic service which infact are on the decline with the rise in the level of economic development.

Other Factors

In his study relating to service sector of developing countries, Sabolo observed that to a great extent, the rapid expansion of employment in the tertiary sector is a fallout of the growth of 'complementary services' such as transport, commerce and the 'new services' such as education and recreation. According to Sabolo (1975: 71), "the demand for 'new' services is the most rapidly growing, while the demand for complementary services grows more slowly and that for 'old services' diminishes in the long run." He argues that purely demographic factors are not responsible for the growth of tertiary sector although they do exercise an indirect influence e.g. through the demand for education and urbanisation. Further, he says that consumption of services in developing countries is 'overdistended' as compared to the stage of development reached due to demonstration effects, imported consumption patterns and a faster growth.

Y. Sabolo has given the following hypotheses for the growth of employment in tertiary sector in developing countries:

Firstly, a preferential consumption of services is responsible for the expansion of employment in this particular sector.

Secondly, this can be attributed to certain characteristics of the production of services. Labour is the most important factor of

---

15. ibid.: 298-99, Table 31.

production in the tertiary sector and there is only limited scope for its substitution by other factors of production like capital and management.

Thirdly, both in developed and developing economies there is an increasing preference among young people and women for service occupations. This can be attributed in the first place to the system of education and in the second place to the availability of many 'feminine occupations' in the tertiary sector as compared to the secondary sector. Further, the preference for employment in this sector is also due to changing trend in the tastes of individuals which has occurred in developed as well as developing countries but seems to be more pronounced in the latter countries. Sabolo (1975: 145) says that the truth is that, "...people are definitely reluctant, largely on account of increasing automation, to spend their working lives adjunct to equipment for the production of goods."

Meier (1970) viewed that a large percentage of workforce (particularly in the developing countries) is engaged in tertiary activities due to a lack of employment opportunities in agriculture or manufacturing sectors because of the use of capital-intensive technology coupled with factor market imperfections and rapid increases in the labour force.

Rottenberg (1953: 169-70) attributes the higher percentage share of services in total employment to the earning structure of underdeveloped economies or to be more precise to the differential prices (i.e. wages) of labour in wage-employment in the production of goods and in own-account/self-employment in the production of services.

Self-employment opportunities are more common in case of services because in many service activities no formal skills are required and the social skills which are required in their case are learned informally and possessed by everyone more or less. On the contrary, in the production of goods certain special skills e.g., occupational and technical skills are required which have to be learned formally and these are not only difficult to acquire but are also possessed by just a few.

Rottenberg points out the difference in the earning structure of the above-mentioned two kinds of employment. He says that in many developed and underdeveloped countries (UDCs), the minimum price of wage employed labour is fixed either formally (by law or formal institutions like trade unions) or informally (by the conscience of the community). But no such prices exist for self-employed labour. Further, in case of the former, price cannot fall to zero or below zero but these possibilities cannot be ruled out for the latter. Moreover, in UDCs the price which is generally paid to the self-employed labour is low compared to the price which is paid to the wage-employed labour. Therefore, it is always worthwhile in these regions (UDCs) to hire labour in self-employed ways. This phenomenon is present in most of the UDCs and accounts for a high proportion of population engaged in services in these regions.

In the opinion of Panchamukhi, Nambiar and Mehta (1986: 236-37) an important factor which has stimulated growth of services sector in developing countries is that the development pattern of these countries has undergone significant changes in the last 15-20 years as economic and social reforms have been undertaken in these economies by their respective governments. With this the modern government has come to play an important role in this respect in the present day world. It tries to mobilise resources both nationally and internationally. Growth, employment generation, poverty alleviation, creating social infrastructure have become the major goals of national economic policies.

Further, they say that "among other reasons that might have stimulated service growth in developing countries are: 1) The historical role of urban middle class in wholesale trade and distribution. 2) The operation of demonstration effect in these countries, creating similar demand patterns to those of high income countries. 3) The comparative advantage of many low-income countries in providing final product services such as tourism. 4) Urbanisation intensified the demand for a wide variety of services ranging from basic infrastructure to general welfare to financial and commercial services" (ibid.)

In the contemporary world, service sector is important for the developing countries because, i) it helps to create more jobs, ii) it economises the use of capital per worker, and iii) it helps in learning new skills by labour, just as in the IT sector.

We may seek another explanation of these observed structural changes. In a study[16] conducted by Economic and Social Council for Asia and the Pacific (ESCAP) and United Nations Industrial Development Organisation (UNIDO) the following explanation has been given for the accelerated growth of services sector and the slower growth of the commodity production sector at a later stage of development. It has been said that the modern S-I-A (share of Services>Industry>Agriculture) corresponds to a relatively high level of economic development. The attainment of this level is a reflection of considerable technological progress, which brings about increased productivity in both industry and agriculture. The relatively high level of productivity in commodity production tends to release labour otherwise bound up in this sphere and makes it available to the services sector. The growth of services sector which provides inputs to the commodity sectors, in turn exerts a favourable effect on productivity in the latter sector. On the demand side, the relatively high and still growing per capita income is accompanied by a shift in demand initially to durable industrial goods and subsequently to services. Thus, both supply and demand factors seem to contribute to a more pronounced shift from commodity production to the service sector at a later stage of development.

Although this argument has been advanced on the basis of the experience of a number of developing ESCAP countries yet this seems to hold true of most developing countries.

Nature and Relative Growth of Tertiary Sector in India

The analysis of structures of production and employment carried out in Chapter 6 clearly shows that the tertiary sector has emerged as the dominant sector of the Indian economy in the decade of the 1990s so far as production structure is concerned. In employment structure too changes have been taking place, though at a slower pace. The share of material production sectors in GDP which stood at 71.53 per cent on an average in the decade of the 1950s declined to 55.78 per cent in the decade of the 1990s. Whereas the share of the tertiary sector increased from 28.09 per cent on an average to 44.22 per cent during the period under consideration.

---

16. ESCAP and UNIDO, 1982: 55.

A question which emerges from the foregoing is what can be the factors behind the growth of tertiary sector in India. These factors have been summed up in Table 2.5 below.

Table 2.5

Plausible Reasons for the Growth of Tertiary Sector of India in 1990s

1. Operation of the Engel's Law in India	Higher demand from domestic consumers, growing demand for services exports from foreign consumers.
2. Growth of Producer Services	Share of producer services in total GDP was 18.91 per cent in 1950-51. It increased to 32.04 per cent in 1990-91 to 2000-01 period.
3. Growth of Consumption Services/Rising Consumerism	Growing demand for entertainment, recreation, education, health, religious services and mushrooming of hotels, restaurants, food joints, fast food centres, eating and drinking places, barber and beauty shops, health spas.
4. Growth of Government Services	Growth of PA&D as a result of Fifth Pay Commission's recommendations.
5. Technological Advancement	Growth of IT, ITES, BPO, TELECOM (Cellular phone services), Financial Services (Credit cards, ATMs, courier, pager services).
6. Liberalisation	Deregulation, Privatisation, opening up to FDI.
7. Demonstration Effect	Growing mobility, growing integration, expansion of foreign trade, growth of tourism, cultural and educational tours.
8. Increasing Urbanisation	Greater demand for infrastructural services, social services and new services .
9. Splintering of Services	Manufacturing is becoming service-oriented.

Sources: The table is based on: Hansda (2002); Gordon and Gupta (2003), and Majumdar (1995).

On the demand side, one of the reasons for growth of services share in GDP can be the growth of final demand for services from both domestic as well as foreign consumers. This rising demand from the domestic consumers gets reflected in a steady rise in private final consumption expenditure on services which rose from 10.2 per cent in 1950-51 to 29.0 per cent in 2000-01 (Hansda, 2002). This points on the one hand towards the operation of Engel's Law of consumption in India and on the other points towards the changes in the demand pattern which were becoming more discernible in 1990s. Rising consumerism too has brought about transformation in the consumption pattern. Growing demand for entertainment, recreation, education, health, religious services and mushrooming of hotels, restaurants, food joints, fast food centres, eating and drinking places, barber and beauty shops, health spas, etc. further support this point. An increase in demand from foreign consumers is clearly reflected in the growing demand for services exports from foreign consumers. In 2002-2003, for the first time the balance of current account became positive for India and 2004-05 is the third consecutive year pointing towards the rising services exports from India. The export of services (in dollars) grew on annual average basis at 9 per cent in the 1980s, 15 per cent in the 1990s and at 21 per cent per annum in the second half of the 1990s. Cumulatively, services exports increased fourfold in the 1990s and reached US$ 25 billion in 2002, about US$7.5 billion of which were software exports (Gordon and Gupta, 2003). During the TE 2003-2005, the share of commercial services exports from India as a share of world export of services stood at 34.8 per cent. Among the five South Asian Countries, India is having revealed comparative advantage in other commercial services which comprises activities such as insurance, financial services, international telecommunications, postal, courier services, business, professional technical, personal, cultural and recreational services, indicating that there exists great potential for export of these services (Joshi, 2005). India has become the services hub and there is dramatic increase in services exports.

Sometimes, the increasing share of services in GDP is attributed to the accounting system i.e. income approach used in this sector (Majumdar, 1995). The salary and wage hike which may be an outcome of general inflation or bargaining power of the white collar workers leads to the enhanced payments without any increase in the real output of this sector. An examination of the issue of faster growth of PA&D sub-sector in the 1980s revealed that the tertiary sector cannot be solely attributed to increase in the growth of GDP originating in PA&D (Nagaraj, 1990; Kapila, 2005). The steep wage hike in 1990s in line with the Fifth Pay Commission's recommendations brought back the issue into focus once again. (Acharya, 2003). During 1997-2001, the services sector growth (at 8.1 per cent) outstripped the industrial sector growth (at 4.8 per cent). Acharya called this phenomenon as 'spurious growth' and partially attributed this growth of services during this period to massive government wage hikes as a result of the Fifth Pay Commission's recommendations. Indeed growth of services sector and that of GDP originated from PA&D Growth as was recognised by the *Economic Survey 1998-99* also. The Survey notes that 'fully one percentage point of growth of 5.0 per cent in GDP for 1997-98 is attributed to the 20 per cent increase in real value added in the PAD sub sector arising chiefly from pay increases to government servants'.

During the period 1997-98 to 1999-2000, the growth in PA&D has been much higher than that of services excluding PA&D, therefore, supporting the fact that PAD indeed has contributed to the overall growth of services. During the post-reform period, an assessment of tertiary sector growth without PAD reflects that PAD is not solely responsible for services growth as the growth of services without PAD was far higher than the growth of PAD. There are other factors which have provided impetus to the growth of tertiary sector.

With liberalisation, growth of services sector has taken place in India. This is because of the reason that as the process of deregulation and privatisation gathers momentum, we open up those areas which were hitherto closed for the private sector. Therefore, the demand for certain services (like that of consultancy services, services of stock brokers) to mobilise the private capital, especially through the capital market has increased. Secondly, as the economy is opened for FDI, the inflow of foreign capital creates a demand for new financial services (like MFs, banking, stock broking, insurance), and real estate services too get a boost. The tenet of liberalisation is to move from a closed to a market economy. Competitive markets increase the demand for a wide range of services varying from advertising to consultancy to market research. The market expands and new areas are covered. Consequently, the demand for leasing services, transport services, auto financing to communication services (courier, pagers, mobiles, postal) also increases.

Another cause of increasing share of services in GDP of India is the operation of demonstration effect because of growing mobility of the population and greater integration of the world economy due to globalisation. Growth of tourism, expansion of foreign trade in services, promotion of cultural and educational tours too are contributing factors (Majumdar, 1995).

Further, increasing urbanisation has led to increase in the demand for infrastructural services, social services and new services, which is accounting for the growth of services sector.

In their paper, Gordon and Gupta (2003) using input-output coefficients and sectoral shares in output tried to find out how important splintering has been in India. Their study reveals that the use of service inputs was much less during early 1990s (the latest input-output matrix for India is available only for 1993-94) than in the 1980s and thus cannot explain the recent pick up in services growth. However, the matrices for different years show that the use of factor inputs in industry and in agriculture increased by about 40 per cent and 150 per cent between 1979-80 and 1993-94 as the input-output coefficient increased from 0.15 to 0.21 in case of the former and 0.02 to 0.05 in case of the latter.

From the foregoing it is clear that the growth of tertiary sector in many developing countries has been taking place in keeping with the so-called Fisher-Clark-Kuznets thesis due to a number of factors.

Conclusions

In this chapter we have seen that when a distinction is made between the broad 'material production sector' and 'tertiary sector' the distinction carries with it a parallel dichotomy of 'productive' and 'unproductive' labour. Classical economists, notably Adam Smith, were of the opinion that only that labour was productive which was engaged in the production of material goods. The services activities were described by them as barren, parasitic and unproductive. Smith's view stuck and resulted in the neglect of this sector for a long time. Smith was later on supported in this respect by Karl Marx, the founder of modern socialism. He revised the Smithian 'Restricted Material Production Concept.' Marxian doctrine has left its deep imprint on national accounting system of the socialists countries where even in the 20th century national income was defined as consisting of only material goods while services were regarded as 'unproductive' and were, therefore, excluded from national income estimates. The importance of the study of the growth of tertiary sector arises from the fact that services sector has been growing at a faster rate than the broad material production sectors in several developing countries or growing quite rapidly in most of them. Therefore, an attempt has been made above to focus on the growth of the tertiary sector *vis-à-vis* material production sectors in the developing countries.

The study of the relative growth of the tertiary sector reveals that there has been taking place a growing 'tertiarisation' of the structures of production and employment in several developing countries. After looking at the long-term changes over 1965-2001-2003 period, it is noted that the process of structural change is underway in many developing countries. Several reasons have been identified for the growth of employment of services sector in developing countries. These are: population pressure, rural-urban migration, growth of complementary and new services, high income elasticity of demand for services, etc. Besides, several basic reasons have been advanced for the relative growth of the services sector. There are primarily two factors, namely, 'supply push' and 'demand induced' factors which account for structural shifts in favour of tertiary sector resulting in substantial growth of employment in tertiary activities.

A notable point is that the growth of tertiary sector *vis-à-vis* material production sectors in many developing countries has been taking place in keeping with the so-called Fisher-Clark-Kuznets thesis. The structural transformation process is a long drawn out one and changes discussed in the preceding sections of this chapter become perceptible only after a fairly long time.

References

Acharya, Shankar (2003). *India's Economy: Some Issues and Answers.* New Delhi: Academic Foundation.

Bhalla, A.S. (1970). "The Role of Services in Employment Expansion", *International Labour Review* 101, Jan.–June.

Cowell, D.W. (1984). *The Marketing of Services.* London: Heinemann.

Datt, Ruddar (2002). "Economic Liberalisation and its Implications for Employment in India" in Ashok Mathur and P.S. Raikhy (eds.), *Economic Liberalisation and its Implications for Employment in India.* New Delhi: Deep and Deep Publications.

ESCAP and UNIDO (1982). "Industrialisation Trends in the Developing ESCAP Region", *Economic Bulletin for Asia and the Pacific,* December.

Fuchs, V.R. (1965). "The Growing Importance of the Service Industries", *The Journal of Businesss of the University of Chicago,* October.

———. (1968). *The Service Economy,* New York: National Bureau of Economic Research.

Galenson, W. (1963). "Economic Development and Sectoral Expansion of Employment", *International Labour Review* 87, June.

Gershuny, Jonathan. I. and Miles, I.D. (1983). *The New Service Economy: The Transformation of Employment in Industrial Societies.* London: Frances Printer Publishers.

Gordon, Jim and Poonam Gupta (2003). "Understanding India's Service Revolution", A Paper prepared for the IMF and NCAER Conference *A Tale of Two Giants: India's and China's Experience with Reform,* November 14-16, New Delhi.

Hansda, Sanjay Kumar (2002). "Services Sector in the Indian Growth Process: Myths and Realities", *The Journal of Income and Wealth* 24(1&2), January-December.

Johnston, B.F. (1971). "Agricultural and Structural Change in Developing Countries: A Survey of Research", *Journal of Economic Literature,* June.

Joshi, Seema (2004). "Tertiary Sector-Driven Growth in India—Impact on Employment and Poverty", *Economic and Political Weekly* 39(37), Sept 11-17.

———. (2005). "GATS, Indian Services Sector and Trade Potential in Health Services" in International Conference on Services Management, Conference Proceedings, Institute for International Management and Technology (IIMT), Haryana, India. pp.192-200.

Kapila, Uma (2005). *Understanding the Problems of Indian Economy.* New Delhi: Academic Foundation

Kuznets, Simon (1966). *Modern Economic Growth.* Calcutta: Oxford and IBH Publishing Co.

Lewis, W.A. (1955). *The Theory of Economic Growth.* London: Novello and Company Ltd.

Majumdar, Krishna (1995). "Dispropotionate Growth of Service Sector in India: 1960-1990", *The Indian Economic Journal* 43(2), October-December.

Marshall, J.N. (1988). *Service and Uneven Development.* Oxford: Oxford University Press.

Marx, Karl (1909). *Das Capital.* Vol. III. Chicago: C.H. Kerr and Co.

———. (1952). *A History of Economic Theories from the Physiocrats to Adam Smith.* New York: The Langland Press.

Meier, G. (1970). "Development without Employment—Note", in G. Meier (ed.), *Leading Issues in Economic Development: Studies in International Poverty.* New York: Oxford University Press.

Nagaraj, R. (1990). "Growth Rate of India's GDP 1950-51 to 1987-88: Examination of Alternative Hypothesis", *Economic and Political Weekly* 24(27). June.

Ofer, Gur (1967). *The Service Industries in a Developing Economy—Israel as a Case Study*. New York: Praeger.

Panchmukhi, V.R., R.G. Nambiar and Rajesh Mehta (1986). "Structural Change and Economic Growth in Developing Countries", *VIII World Economic Congress of the International Economic Association*, Theme 4, December.

Rottenberg, Simon (1953). "Note on Economic Progress and Occupational Distribution", *Review of Economics and Statistics*, May.

Sabolo, Yves (1975). *Service Industries*. Geneva: International Labour Office.

Schoell, W.F. and J.T. Ivy (1981). *Marketing: Contemporary Concepts and Practices*, Mass: Allyn and Bacon. p.277.

Smith, Adam (1910). *An Enquiry into the Nations and Causes of the Wealth of Nations*. Vol. II, Chap. III. London: Dent.

Studenski, Paul (1958). *The Income of Nations, Theory, Measurement and Analysis: Past and Present*. New York: University Press. p.19&21.

Thomas, Jayam Jose (2005). "New Technologies for India's Development", in Kirit S. Parikh and R. Radhakrishna (eds.), *India's Development Report 2004-05*. New Delhi: Oxford Universty Press.

Tucker, K.A. (1977). *Economics of Australian Service Sector*. London: Croom Helm Ltd.

Walters, C.G. and B.J. Bergiel (1982). *Marketing Channels*. Scott, Foresman, Glenview, Ill. p.483.

Wilczynki, J. (1970). *The Economics of Socialism*. George Allen and Unwin Ltd.

World Bank (1993). *World Development Report*. New York: Oxford University Press.

This chapter was originally published as an article in 2006. "Tertiary Sector in Developing Economies—Its Nature and Relative Growth" in V.N. Upadhyay *et al.* (eds.), *Productivity and Quality: A Multidisciplinary Perspective*. New Delhi: Tata McGraw Hill Publishers.

3

Composition of Tertiary Sector

Inter-Temporal Changes

Introduction

In several of our studies elsewhere we have (Joshi, 2004a; 2004b; 2005a; 2005b; 2006) provided a strong evidence of the fact that the service sector has been growing faster than the commodity producing sectors in most of the developing economies. The continuously increasing share of the services sector in GDP and employment of the developing as well as developed economies of the world has led to a controversy. According to one school of thought, this relative growth of the sector is desirable while the other school argues that it is undesirable (Joshi, 2005a). In the present chapter, we shall deal with another debate, *viz.* what actually constitutes the services sector. In fact no single, unambiguous and unanimously accepted definition of this sector has emerged so far. We shall first of all present an overview of the main classifications of the tertiary sector. Subsequently, we shall focus on inter-temporal changes in the composition of the tertiary sector. We would also highlight in brief the emergence of new services and their role in the Indian economy. Finally, we shall discuss the flip side of the growth of IT and ITES before concluding the discussion of this chapter.

Emerging Components of the Tertiary Sector —A Review[1]

We shall review below the various classifications of the tertiary sector so as to notice what constitutes the services sector. The analysis

1. This and the next but one part of this chapter are based on "From Conventional to New Services: Broadened Scope of Tertiary Sector", *Indian Journal of Labour Economics*, April-June, 2006.

of services has suffered from definitional and classificatory problems. More than three decades ago Stiglar (1956) remarked that, "There exists no authoritative consensus on either the boundaries or the classification of the service industries." Fuchs (1968) after making 'careful review of subsequent studies' found no basis for challenging this conclusion.

Unfortunately no single, precise, unquestionable and unanimously accepted definition of services sector has emerged so far. In different empirical studies, this sector has been defined in different ways. Even the definitions of this particular sector as given by the two-founding fathers of the three-sector model i.e., Fisher and Clark are not identical. The former defined tertiary sector as consisting of "transport, communication, trade, government, personal and domestic services, and in some versions construction" (Kindleberger and Herick, 1977). On the other hand, the latter opines that this sector covers " all forms of economic activity not included under primary and secondary"[2] and he later listed "distribution, transport, public administration, domestic services and all other activities producing a non-material output" (Clark, 1940) as the principal tertiary activities.

Further, the inclusion and exclusion of certain activities like transport, communication and public utilities (i.e., electricity, gas and water supply) has also been a subject of controversy. Fuchs points out[3] that while some writers like Ofer (1967) have included the foregoing activities in their studies, some others like Lengelle (1966), and Stigler (1956) have excluded them in their respective studies,[4] still there are others like Worton (1969) who have included in their study only the first two of these activities i.e., transport and communication and have excluded the third one i.e., public utilities. This composition of the sector was later used by Deakin and George (1965) and Dowie (1966) in their studies of services sector relating to UK and Australia, respectively.

Besides, even within the work of a single author, variations in definitions can be noticed. In this context Fuch quotes the example of

2. Quoted from Fisher, 1939: 36 and also see Colin, 1939: 13.
3. This and the following paragraphs are based on Fuchs, 1968: 14-15.
4. However, Fuchs who defined service industries in juxtaposition to goods industries, himself excluded transportation, communications and public utilities from the service sector placed them in the industry sector because of their heavy dependence upon capital equipment and complex technology.

Simon Kuznets who in an article published in 1958 included transportation, communications and public utilities in the service sector but excluded them in his later work, *viz.*, *Modern Economic Growth*. In this latter work he defined the services sector as comprising "trade, finance, real estate, personal, domestic, professional and government services" (Kuznets, 1966).

Foote and Hatt (1953: 365) have suggested the classification of the service industries into three categories: 'Tertiary', 'Quaternary' and 'Quinary'.

In the first category they include domestic and quasi-domestic services: restaurants and hotels, barber and beauty shops, laundry and dry cleaning establishments, repair and maintenance services and handicrafts once performed at home.

The 'Quaternary' category in their opinion is made up of finance and administration and transportation, communication and commerce. Their most noticeable characteristic being that they ' facilitate and effectuate the division of labour'.

They clubbed together activities such as health care, education and recreation (including the arts) in the 'Quinary' industry. They maintain that services rendered by this subsector are designed to change and 'improve' the recipient in some way. They say that services rendered by the 'Tertiary industry' is intended to maintain the customers in the style to which they are accustomed to but the services comprised in this sector are devoted to the cultivation of behaviour to which they are not accustomed to.

M.A. Katouzian in an article (1970) has provided the following classification of the service sector. He analyses the growth pattern of this sector by dividing it into three categories: New services, Complementary Services and Old Services.

According to him, new services are those which have experienced a great shift in demand with the advent of 'high mass consumption' and thereafter. Their consumption seems to be an increasing function of per capita income and leisure time. It includes such subsectors of the economy as education, consumption of modern clinical and medical services, entertainment in general (including holiday resorts, hotels and restaurants, etc.).

In the complementary services Katouzian includes services whose production normally takes a sharp turn with the rise of manufacturing production (and 'the take-off of the rate of growth of output in general). It includes intermediary services like banking, finance, transportation, wholesale and retail trade that are of a complementary nature to the production process.

Old services, on the other hand, consist of those activities which flourished before industrialisation and whose importance and contribution has almost continuously declined since. Domestic services are included in this category.

H.L. Browning and J. Singlemann (Gershuny and Miles, 1983) have offered an alternative classification of the service sector in which they have divided service industry into four categories, *viz.*, distributive, producer, social and personal services. They renamed the conventional primary and secondary sectors as 'extractive' and 'transformative'. Table 3.1 shows the Browning-Singlemann classification of services.

Some writers defined services in terms of their characteristics (Hill, 1977), some in the form of transaction involved (Sampson and Snape, 1985) and some others like Bhagwati (Giarini, 1987) categorised them into groups.[5] Robert Inman's (1985) classification of services is given in Table 3.2.[6]

In this modern age of IT, information is becoming a fourth factor of production in addition to land, labour and capital. It is viewed as a raw material of knowledge as wood is for making of a table. It is also argued that the four sector model comprising of Information related services in addition to primary, secondary and tertiary sector may be evolving. This would consist of information, knowledge, arts and ethics. The activities of generating, processing, transmitting, disseminating, storing, archiving and retrieving information constitutes an information industry (Low, 2000).

Bhattacharya and Mitra (1997) in their study relating to composition of tertiary sector in 48 developing and industrialised countries pointed out that the workers in a particular industry division do not carry out a single type of activity. Therefore, they decomposed

---

5. Joshi, 2005b: 193.

6. Unni and Uma Rani, 2000: 803-827.

Table 3.1

Browning-Singlemann Classification of the Service Sector

1. Distributive Service	
i)	Transportation and Storage
ii)	Communication
iii)	Wholesale Trade
iv)	Retail Trade (except eating and drinking places)
2. Producer Services	
v)	Banking, Credit, and Other Financial Services
vi)	Insurance
vii)	Real Estate
viii)	Engineering and Architectural Services
ix)	Accounting and Book Keeping
x)	Miscellaneous Business Services
xi)	Legal Services
3. Social Services	
xii)	Medical and Health Services
xiii)	Hospitals
xiv)	Education
xv)	Welfare and Religious Services
xvi)	Non-Profit Organisations
xvii)	Postal Services
xviii)	Government
xix)	Miscellaneous Professional and Social Services
4. Personal Services	
xx)	Domestic Services
xxi)	Hostels and Lodging Places
xxii)	Eating and Drinking Places
xxiii)	Repair Services
xxiv)	Laundry and Dry Cleaning
xxv)	Barber and Beauty Shops
xxvi)	Entertainment and Recreational Services
xxvii)	Miscellaneous Personal Services

Source: Gershuny and Miles, 1983.

tertiary sector workers into four occupational categories depending upon the nature of activities they perform. They divided occupational classes into four major groups *viz.*, bureaucratic services, distributive services, consumer services and producer services (Table 3.3).

Table 3.2

Robert Inman's Classification of Services

Classification of Services	*Characteristics*	*Examples*
1. Stagnant Personal Services	High quality, correlation with the labour time spent	Haircutting, teaching, live artistic performance
2. Progressive Impersonal Services	a) Immense dependence on electronic technology b) No contact between the producers and consumers c) High Technology and productivity growth	Telecommunication and multimedia
3. Asymptomatically Impersonal Services	Productivity growth self-extinguishing	Broadcasting, computation and R&D.

Source: Inman, 1985.

Table 3.3

Bhattacharya-Mitra (B-M) Classification of Tertiary Sector Workers

1.	**Bureaucratic Services**
i)	Professionals
ii)	Technical and Related Workers
iii)	Administrative and Managerial Workers
iv)	Clerical and Related Workers
2.	**Distributive Services**
i)	All Sales Workers
3.	**Consumer Services**
i)	Service Workers
4.	**Producers Services**
i)	Workers Engaged in Agriculture, Animal Husbandary and Forestry
ii)	Fisher Men and Hunters
iii)	Production and Related Workers
iv)	Transport Equipment Operators and Labourers in the Tertiary Sector

Source: Bhattacharya and Mitra, 1997.

In WTO classification, services have been classified into the following 12 sectors:

Thus, the brief review of the definitions of the tertiary sector and the three treatments of services as shown above confirms the fact that due to lack of universally accepted theoretical framework for defining

Table 3.4

Classification of Services Sector under WTO

1.	Business (including Professional and Computer) Services
2.	Communication (including Postal, Courier, Telecom) Services
3.	Construction and Related Engineering Services
4.	Distributive Services
5.	Educational Services
6.	Environmental Services
7.	Financial (Insurance and Banking) Services
8.	Health-related and Social Services
9.	Tourism and Trade Related Services
10.	Recreational, Cultural and Sporting Services
11.	Transport Services
12.	Other Services not included elsewhere

Source: UNCTAD/WTO (1999).

services, considerable ambiguity still prevails concerning this concept. There obviously arises a need for some standard classification, which should not only promote the uniformity and standardisation in accounts but should also improve the reliability of comparative data. These above-mentioned points formed the main objectives of the United Nations System of National Accounts when United Nations took up the question of evolving systematic National Income accounting after World War II. The UN System of National Accounts (SNA, 1968) recommends that for preparing national income statistics all the economic activities of the nation should be classified according to the International Standard Industrial Classification of economic activities (ISIC, 1968) which is shown in Table 3.5.

In the National Income Accounting system in India, the tertiary sector includes the following sub-sectors:

1. Trade, Hotels and Restaurants
    - 1.1 Trade
    - 1.2 Hotels and restaurants
2. Transport, Storage and Communication
    - 2.1 Railways
    - 2.2 Transport by Other Means

2.3 Storage

2.4 Communication

3. Financing, Insurance, Real Estate and Business Services

3.1 Banking and Insurance

3.2 Real Estate, Ownership of Dwellings and Business Services

4. Community, Social and Personal Services

4.1 Public Administration and Defence

4.2 Other services

Table 3.5

United Nations Classification of Economic Activities

Sector	*Economic Activity*	*International Standard Industrial Classification Indicators*
Primary	Agriculture, hunting, forestry, fishing	1
Secondary	Mining and quarrying, manufacturing, electricity, gas, water, construction	2-5
Tertiary	Wholesale and retail trade, restaurants and hotels, transport, storage and communication, financing, insurance, real estate and business services, community, social and personal services, activities not adequately defined	6-0

Source: United Nations, 1968.

It is quite obvious from the above discussion that services comprise many diverse and heterogeneous activities and, therefore, arriving at a precise and universally accepted definition appears to be an uphill task. Since ICT driven globalisation, WTO and GATS have further widened the scope of services to include new services also, the task appears to be even more difficult.

From the foregoing, we may conclude that services sector comprises a wide spectrum of low productivity activities (mainly in the informal sector like repair and maintenance services, transport, shoe-shine, cobblers, hawkers, personal services like hair dresser, washermen, etc.) and high productivity activities (mainly professional, legal, etc.), new services like software, IT (internet), IT enabled services (like call centres, design, business process outsourcing), cellular phone services (telecommunication), ATMs, credit cards, etc. (financial services) as well (Joshi, 2004a).

Composition of Tertiary Sector—Inter-Temporal Changes

The historical development of the use of the term tertiary sector, its definitions and Smithian and Marxian perspectives on productive and unproductive labour were discussed by us in a research paper (Joshi, 2006). Here, we shall take up yet another important aspect of services sector in developing economies, *viz.*, structural changes which have occured within the services sector. The ensuing discussion focuses on the inter-temporal changes in the composition of services sector in the developing economies. The discussion has been divided into analysis of the structure of services output and employment by industry group.

Changes in the Composition of Services Sector Output—1970–2000-01

Table 3.6 shows the changes in the shares of sub-sectors in overall tertiary sector output in selected developing economies over the 1970–2000-01 period. We have taken a sample of 24 countries for this purpose from a publication of the United Nations.

We observe from the Table that during the 1970–2000-01 period, out of a sample of 24 countries, the share of 'community, social and personal services' component of tertiary output increased in largest number of countries (87.5 per cent) indicating that attention was being paid to the development of social infrastructural facilities in these developing economies so as to satisfy the growth requirements of the complementary secondary sector. This was followed by 'transport, storage and communication' and 'finance, insurance, real estate and business services' which recorded an increase in their shares in 45.8 per cent and 41.7 per cent countries respectively. The next was 'wholesale and retail trade, restaurants and hotels' sub-head accounting for an increase in its share in tertiary output in 16.6 per cent countries.

Though among these four major divisions of services sector, the share of the last mentioned division, *viz.*, 'wholesale and retail trade, restaurants and hotels, increased in the least number of countries, yet the figures in the Table reveal that in the year 2000-01, 79.2 per cent countries accounted for its highest share in overall tertiary output. It was followed by finance, insurance, real estate and business services and 'community, social and personal services' (25 per cent) countries each.

It is important to point out here that in none of the countries did 'transport, storage and communication, make the highest contribution to total tertiary output in either of the years. The GDP originating from the services sector as a whole increased in 91.7 per cent countries shown in Table 3.6.

From the above, it is clear that the share of transport, storage and communication sub-sector in total tertiary sector output increased in the largest number of countries (79.2 per cent). The rise in the share of this sub-sector reflects the expansion of economic infrastructure in these economies because infrastructure is the basic input required for the growth of the economy and also for sustaining that growth. If the base is not developed, the superstructure cannot be built up. This has been happening in India as well in the later half of the 1990s. Even though high growth rates of GDP have been attained, yet these growth rates are not sustainable in view of the infrastructural bottlenecks present in the economy.

Table 3.7 gives relative shares of sub-sectors of service sector in overall Gross Domestic Product (GDP) at constant prices for the years 1970 and 2000-01 which have been ranked by the order of percentage share figures. We have taken the same sample of 24 countries as in the preceding Table and have borrowed the data from the source mentioned there. The following main points emerge from the data in the Table:

(i) 'Wholesale and retail trade, restaurants and hotels' was the main service activity in most of the developing countries in both the years. The percentage number of countries where these services ranked first stood at 79.2 per cent in 1970 and 52.2 per cent in 2000-01.

(ii) The group comprising 'finance, insurance, real estate and business services' occupied second rank in 54.2 per cent countries. However, the percentage number of countries getting the second rank declined from 54.2 per cent to 20.8 per cent over the 30-year period.

Table 3.6

Composition of Tertiary Sector Output-Inter-Temporal Changes

Sr. No.	Country	Period	Wholesale & Retail Trade, Restaurants & Hotels	Transport, Storage & Communication	Finance, Insurance, Real Estate & Business Services	Community, Social & Personal Services	Tertiary Output as a Percentage of Total Output
1.	Malaysia	1970	43	18.6	30.9	7.5	27.87
		2000	28.86	16.66	35.1	19.38	52.25
2.	Mexico	1970	51.1	9.3	22.7	16.9	50.7
		2000	31.84	16.43	22.62	29.1	63.1
3.	Myanmar	1970	37.4	8.7	3.1	50.8	49.9
		1970	45.21	13.87	8.11	32.8	51.84
4.	Morocco	1970	74.2	10.8	1.6	13.4	37.8
		1998	52.14	15.38	5.07	27.41	40.38
5.	Nicaragua	1970	49.7	12.6	21.9	15.8	43.4
		2001	44.17	11.94	17.14	26.74	39.17
6.	Pakistan	1970	43	18.7	16.8	21.5	29.3
		2001	29.65	19.88	16.68	33.79	46.91
7.	Panama	1970	39	14.8	29.6	16.5	46.91
		2000	25.17	20.1	35.38	19.35	75.29
8.	Paraguay	1970	28.5	18.3	16.7	36.6	21.7
		1996	55.32	9.89	5.7	31.18	47.8
9.	Peru	1970	47.6	14.3	28.4	9.7	36
		2000	34.25	15.02	22.46	28.26	53.35
10.	Puerto Rico	1970	42.8	11.8	32.6	12.7	49
		2000	26.48	11.99	34.9	26.63	70.18
11.	Singapore	1970	42.6	13.9	32.2	11.3	51.7
		2001	25.86	15.11	41.93	17.1	74.6
12.	South Africa	1970	33.3	22.8	39.7	4.2	28.6
		2001	22.39	18.6	31.93	27.07	55.69

Contd...

...contd..

Sr. No.	*Country*	*Period*	*Wholesale & Retail Trade, Restaurants & Hotels*	*Transport, Storage & Communication*	*Finance, Insurance, Real Estate & Business Services*	*Community, Social & Personal Services*	*Tertiary Output as a Percentage of Total Output*
13.	Sri Lanka	1970	53.7	26.4	11.3	8.6	32.8
		2001	42.56	20.71	15.54	21.19	52.22
14.	Syrian Arab Rep.	1970	53	24.6	17.1	5.3	43
		2001	36.56	30.03	7.86	25.55	42.47
15.	Thailand	1970	52	14.9	19.3	14	4.3
		2000	40.44	21.26	14.92	23.38	45.54
16.	Trinidad & Tobago	1970	40	30.2	15.6	14.2	47.6
		2001	22.95	14.75	23.77	38.52	51.05
17.	Tunisia	1970	39.2	17.9	19.2	23.7	34
		2001	28.09	19.32	10.5	42.1	50.11
18.	Turkey	1970	36.5	22.3	35	6.3	36.6
		1997	45.79	26.53	14.76	12.92	48.3
19.	Uganda	1970	47.1	17.6	29.4	5.9	23.3
		1999	38.6	13.86	26.83	20.72	35.03
20.	Uruguay	1970	46.1	15.4	27	11.6	37.4
		2001	20.31	18.22	38.1	23.4	65.45
21.	Venezuela	1970	27.1	26.1	36.1	10.7	39.5
		2001	24.84	15.3	29.24	30.61	42.76
22.	Yemen	1970	59.5	11.8	25.2	3.5	25.3
		2000	15.18	15.1	15.54	54.18	47.83
23.	Zambia	1970	48	16.4	31.5	4.1	22
		2000	38.86	12.14	34.15	14.84	52
24.	Zimbabwe	1970	28.6	19.2	16	14.84	38.3
		1999	34.2	17.9	12.1	35.9	46.1

Source: The percentages are computed by us from United Nations. *National Accounts Statistics: Main Aggregates and Detailed Tables, 1990,* Part II. 1992. New York. and Ibid., Part II. 2001.

(iii) The sub-sector 'transport, storage and communication' got the penultimate rank. The figures stood at 66.7 per cent in 1970 and 37.5 per cent in 2000-01.

(iv) The sub-sector 'community, social and personal services' seems to be relatively less important in the sample developing countries as it occupied the last rank in 58.3 per cent countries in the year 1970. But the percentage number of countries getting the fourth rank declined from 58.3 per cent to as low as 8.3 per cent during the period under study.

We notice from the above that though the subdivisions: 'trade, restaurants and hotels', 'finance, insurance, real estate and business services', 'transport, storage and communication' and 'community, social and personal services' captured the first, second, third and fourth ranks respectively in highest percentage of countries in the year 1970, yet a noteworthy fact is that the percentage number of countries under each of these three ranks has registered a decline subsequently.

Changes in the Structure of Service Sector Employment, 1975-2001

After having discussed the changes in the composition of services sector output, now we will observe the significant and noticeable intrasectoral structural changes which have taken place in services sector in terms of employment.

In Table 3.8 we have taken a sample of 19 developing countries for which complete and adequate data on sub-sectors of the services sector for the period 1975-2001 was available in 1982 and 2004 issues of the *Yearbook of Labour Statistics* published by the International Labour Organisation. The Table shows the characteristics of the employment structure of tertiary sector of these developing economies. Although we are aware that the sample of developing economies taken here is too small to be representative of the group, yet lack of adequate data for a larger group of countries obliged us to depend on this small sample.

A look at Table 3.8 shows that in these developing economies the service employment taking place in 'finance, insurance, real estate and business services' subhead increased in 77.8 per cent countries. The next in importance was 'trade, restaurants and hotels' sub-sector which

Table 3.7

Rank Order and Product Shares of Service Activities

Activity	*Rank I*		*Rank II*		*Rank III*		*Rank IV*	
	1970	*2000*	*1970*	*2000*	*1970*	*2000*	*1970*	*2000*
Wholesale and Retail Trade, Hotels and Restaurants	19 (79.2)	12 (52.2)	5	6	-	6	-	-
Transport, Storage and Communication	-	-	3	2	16 (66.7)	9 (37.5)	5	13 (54.2)
Finance, Insurance, Real estate and Business Services	2	6	13 (54.2)	5	4	4	5	9
Community, Social and Personal Services	3	6	3	11 (45.8)	4	5	14 (58.3)	2

Note: 1. Due to non-availability of data for the year 2000 in case of some countries data varying between 1996-2001 have been used.

2. Figures in parentheses show the percentage number of countries capturing different ranks in two different time periods.

Source: United Nations. *National Accounts Statistics: Main Aggregates and Detailed Tables, 1990,* Part II. 1992. New York. and Ibid., Part II. 2001.

accounted for an increase in its share in total tertiary sector employment in 55.6 per cent countries. However, the share of this sub-head declined in rest of the countries. Interestingly, the remaining two sub-sectors, namely, 'transport, storage and communication' and 'community, social and personal services' registered an increase and decrease in their shares in tertiary sector employment by 33.3 per cent and 27.8 per cent in case of the former and 61.1 per cent and 66.7 per cent countries in case of the latter respectively.

During the period under reference, employment taking place in the tertiary sector as a whole recorded an increase in 83.3 per cent countries. This can be mainly attributed to 'finance, insurance, real estate and business services' as the service sector employment originating from this particular sub-sector showed an upward trend in 77.8 per cent countries in absolute numbers.

In Table 3.9 above we have shown the rank order and relative sizes of service activities in total employment. The following points emerge from this Table:

Table 3.8

Sub-Sectoral Structure of Service Employment (1975-76 to 2001-02)

(Percentage of Total Service Sector Labour)

S.No.	Country	Period	Wholesale & Retail Trade, Restaurants & Hotels	Transport, Storage & Communication	Finance, Insurance, Real Estate & Business Services	Community, Social & Personal Services	Tertiary Output as a Percentage of Total Output
1.	Bolivia	1975	22.7	17.5	0.8	59	33.4
		2001	51.9	11.3	9.1	27.7	42.6
2.	Botswana	1975	29.2	5.6	5.7	59.4	61.1
		2001	30.6	6.3	12.5	50.6	53.6
3.	Brasil	1975	33.4	18	10.1	38.5	42.1
		2001	24	7.1	3	65.9	59.4
4.	Chile	1975	27.8	12.3	5	55	52.6
		2001	30.1	12.8	12.1	45	62.5
5.	Costa Rica	1976	33.7	9.4	5.3	51.6	42
		2001	40.2	9.2	13	37.7	60.5
6.	Egypt	1975	29	14.5	2.9	53.7	32.1
		2001	28	13	6.1	52.8	49.9
7.	Honduras	1975	34	12.3	3.4	50.2	23.5
		2001	14.8	68.2	9.1	8.1	35.1
8.	Hongkong	1975	64.4	8	12	15.6	41
		2001	37.6	13.5	18.3	30.1	80.3
9.	Israel	1975	20.6	12.2	11.2	56	59.3
		2001	24.1	9.1	21.5	45.2	72.3

Contd...

...*contd*...

Sr. No.	*Country*	*Period*	*Wholesale & Retail Trade, Restaurants & Hotels*	*Transport, Storage & Communication*	*Finance, Insurance, Real Estate & Business Services*	*Community, Social & Personal Services*	*Tertiary Output as a Percentage of Total Output*
10.	Korea, Rep of	1975	52.2	10	4.2	33.6	30.4
		2001	44.2	10	17.3	28.5	61.5
11.	Nicaragua	1975	24.2	7.4	8.8	59.7	63
		2001	43.1	8.1	3.5	45.3	38.2
12.	Pakistan	1975	42	18.4	2.5	37	26.4
		2001	40.3	15	2.4	42.3	33.5
13.	Panama	1975	27.8	10.5	6.4	55.3	46.9
		2001	38.7	13.5	9.8	38	58.9
14.	Puerto Rico	1975	30.5	7.1	4.1	58.3	64.8
		2001	27.1	5.1	4.7	63.1	76.4
15.	Sri Lanka	1975	50.1	31.4	9.6	9	19.6
		2001	41.4	12	6.5	40.1	35.3
16.	Turkey	1975	27.1	20	3.1	49.8	21.8
		2001	44.5	12.3	8.3	34.9	39
17.	Uruguay	1976	25.3	12.2	9	53.5	64.5
		2001	35.6	9.9	14.4	40.1	62.8
18.	Venezuela	1975	34.1	10.3	6.4	49.2	54.9
		2001	38.3	10.2	7.5	44	68.2

Source: International Labour Office. *Yearbook of Labour Statistics*, 1982; 2004.

Table 3.9

Rank Order and Employment Share of Service Activities

Activity	*Rank I*		*Rank II*		*Rank III*		*Rank IV*	
	1975-76	*2001-02*	*1975-76*	*2001-02*	*1975-76*	*2001-02*	*1975-76*	*2001-02*
Trade, Restaurants and Hotels	4 (22.2)	7 (38.9)	14 (77.8)	11 (61.1)	-	-	-	-
Transport, Storage and Communications	-	1 (5.6)	1 (5.6)	-	14 (77.8)	11 (61.1)	3 (16.7)	6 (33.3)
Finance, Insurance, Real Estate and Business Services	-	-	-	-	4 (22.2)	7 (38.9)	14 (77.8)	11 (61.1)
Community, Social and Personal Services	14 (77.8)	10 (55.6)	3 (16.7)	7 (38.9)	-	-	1 (5.6)	1 (5.6)

Note: Figures in parentheses show the percentage number of countries capturing different ranks in two different time periods.

Source: International Labour Office. *Yearbook of Labour Statistics*, 1982; 2004.

(i) In terms of employment, the 'community, social and personal services' was the main service activity in 77.8 per cent of the countries in 1975-76. The position of this sub-sector declined relatively in 2001-02 when it captured the first rank in a smaller percentage of countries i.e. 55.6 per cent countries. What merits attention here is the fact that during the period under consideration, only in one country each did this sub-sector occupy the fourth rank. It got the second rank in 36.8 per cent countries in 2000-01 and is none of the countries did this sector occupy the third rank.

(ii) 'Trade, restaurants and hotels' captured the second rank in 77.8 per cent countries in 1975 and 57.9 per cent countries in 2000-01 and consequently emerged as the second important employment provider. This is so because the wholesale and retail trade sub-sector renders services which require relatively little capital equipment and is more labour intensive.

(iii) In rank order, 'transport, storage and communications' occupied the penultimate rank in largest number of countries in 1975-76 as well as 2000-01.

(iv) Amongst the four sub-groups of services producing sectors 'finance, insurance, real estate and business services' seems to be of relatively less importance because this sub-head got the last rank in 77.8 per cent countries in 1975-76 and 61.1 per cent countries in 2000-01. It is important to point out here that during the period under reference in none of the countries this sub-sector got the first rank. This was in sharp contrast to the 'community, social and personal services' division which as pointed out earlier occupied the first rank in most of the countries.

We also notice from the Table above that the shares of the two sub-sectors, *viz.*, 'community, social and personal services', and 'trade, restaurants and hotels' varied considerably from country to country as compared to the other two sub-sectors, namely, 'finance, insurance, real estate and business services' and 'transport, storage and communications'. Besides, the size of 'finance, insurance, real estate and business services' division in total employment has been observed to be relatively small particularly in comparison with the size of the 'community, social and personal services' and 'trade, restaurants and hotels' divisions.

It can be concluded from this discussion that the overall pattern outlined above reflects the difference between, 'producer services' and 'final consumption services'. The former category of services is in the nature of intermediate inputs to final production in the primary and secondary sectors or is associated with marketing of the material output in the form of, say, business services, legal and consultancy services, public relations, quality control, accountancy and distribution, etc. Such producer services are clubbed under the heading 'finance, insurance, real estate and business services'. These producer services on the whole require higher training and educational qualifications than final consumption services. The latter services do not serve as inputs in any formal production process and are directly sold to the consumers for their personal use. Its examples are: marketed services like entertainment and leisure services, personal services such as hairdressing and the like and some non-marketed services such as education and medical services. The size of the 'finance, insurance, real estate and business services' is associated with the level of economic development already attained. That is why we notice that in many developing countries, its size was very small, but has risen as compared to the size of the other sub-sectors during the period of the survey taken by us.

Besides the above explanation, the difference in percentage share of each of the sub-sectors in sectoral employment can also be explained in terms of capital-intensive and labour-intensive nature of each of these activities. The 'finance, insurance, real estate and business services' sub-division of services sector is relatively capital- intensive in nature, whereas the 'community, social and personal services' and 'trade, restaurants and hotels' segments are relatively more labour-intensive and, therefore, require more labour per unit of capital. The latter two activities are, therefore, the main employment providers in most of the developing countries, and are also perhaps of a residual labour absorbing nature.

From the above discussion, we notice certain points of difference in the structural change within the service sector in terms of GDP and employment. We observe that in total tertiary-sector output, the share of 'community, social and personal services' sub-head increased in the largest number of countries, indicating that the requirements of growth of material production induced or provided the basis for development of social infrastructural facilities in these developing countries.

We also notice that though the share of 'finance, insurance, real estate and business services' in total tertiary sector employment recorded an increase in 41.7 per cent countries, yet the size of this sub-head was still small compared to the size of the other sub-sectors. The reason may have been that the size of this particular sub-sector is associated with the level of economic development attained. The higher the level of economic development, the larger would be its size and *vice versa*. Another reason is that these service activities are relatively capital and skill intensive in nature, and most developing countries still being low or middle income countries, could not afford 'the needed' amount of capital and skill to develop this sub-sector adequately.

The foregoing analysis of relative size of services activities in total GDP and employment and their arrangement in rank order shows that in terms of GDP 'wholesale and retail trade, restaurants and hotels' was the main service activity in most of the developing countries. The sub-sector 'community, social and personal services' which appeared to be of relatively less importance in terms of GDP, was observed to be the major employment provider in most of the developing countries in 1975-76 and 2001-02. This is mainly because of the reason that activities included under this sub-division are relatively more labour-intensive in nature and require little capital equipment. About this sub-sector, we also hypothesised earlier that it has perhaps played the role of residual labour absorbing group of activities in the face of (a) rural to urban migration, and (b) relative lack of employment growth in other tertiary activities and secondary sector.

These foregoing analysis of structural changes observed within the services sector is rather tentative in nature, because the number of countries included in the two sets of data taken by us, i.e. 24 and 18 countries is too small to yield reliable results. Hopefully, these changes broadly indicate what has been happening in most developing economies. Let us now try to find out what has been happening to the composition of tertiary sector in India.

Emergence and Role of New Services in the Indian Economy[7]

Before taking up the role of new services in the Indian economy, it would be very important to emphasise here that 'servicisation' of the Indian economy has taken place over almost 57 years of the planning era (for details see Chapter 6).

Its is well-known now that the Information Communication Technologies (ICTs) are the driving force of globalisation. It is being seen as the new engine of growth. The recent surge in services during the last two decades has been attributed mainly to high productivity services such as Information Technology (IT) services and Information Technology Enabled Services (ITES). As per the National Association of Software and Service Companies (NASSCOM)—the premier chamber of commerce and 'voice' of the software and Business Process Outsourcing

---

7. This section is based on Anonymous, 2004; 2005a; 2005b; 2005c; Joshi, 2004; Mehra, 2005; Karnik, 2005; *www.nasscom.org; Economic Survey 2004–2005.*

(BPO) in India[8]—the service sector would provide 10 million jobs by 2009 provided further liberalisation of services sector continues and secondly, if India takes leverage of this powerful diplomatic tool internationally to get skilled Indians into overseas markets, easing visa restrictions and as in merchandise, secures market share for India's brains, and in the process induces investment into India. The Global Services Coalition comprising a premier league of countries has joined forces to put services i.e knowledge-intensive industry on the international map. India's NASSCOM is a part of it. The point put forth by this group is: the Doha round cannot be closed until the services are meted out the same treatment as agriculture. Seeing robust growth of this sector and its vast export and revenue earning potential, it is being felt now that this powerful component should be used while negotiating with the rest of the world in forums like the WTO. Recently, Mr. Sunil Mehta, vice president, NASSCOM submitted a draft on India's offer on GATS to the Ministry of Commerce. It is also felt that we must shift from bilateral agreements in services to multilateral spheres, otherwise other countries might use it as a leverage tool *vis-à-vis* India during trade talks. We cannot ignore the fact that services is a particular facet of India's new Free Trade Agreements with other countries.[9]

Telecom sector in India has shown spectacular success since 1991 and especially after the New Telecom Policy of 1999, which introduced liberalisation and private sector participation in this sector. Besides, measures like formation of Telecom Regulatory Authority of India in 1997 with a purpose to provide an independent and fair regulatory regime to ensure competition and protect consumer interest and Amended Telecom Regulatory Authority of India Act 2000 to ensure level playing field in telecom and its regulation has provided a conducive environment for growth of this sector. Further, setting up of National Task Force on Information Technology and Software Development in May 1998 which recommended, among other things, 'IT for All', and the constitution of Working Group on Information Technology for the Masses in May 2000 by the Government of India. Introduction of IT legislations in almost all states, thrust on R&D are

8. See Anonymous, 2005a: 18.

9. Anonymous, 2005b: 19.

other progressive state measures to provide a boost to this sector. There has been a telecommunication revolution ongoing in virtually all sectors. In 1948, there were only 80,000 telephone connections in India, their number increased to one million in 1971, two million in 1981, five million in 1991 and more than 10 million in April, 2005. Teledensity is just short of 10 per 100-population. All these facts and figures point towards the opportunities that exist for service providers.

Mobile phones are no longer considered to be a luxury anymore. There has been phenomenal growth of mobile telephony in India in recent years. This can be contributed to the pragmatic policy of shifting fixed license-free contracts to revenue-sharing and opening up competition, and TRAI's consumer interest interventions. All these measures led to a huge reduction in service charges and handset costs with improved coverage and services.[10]

Though we lag behind the world in teledensity and broadband connectivity, yet 'catching up' is underway with the launching of the Broadband Policy of October 14, 2004 claims *Economic Survey 2004-2005*. The policy aims at targeting 3 million Internet subscribers and 20 million Broadband subscribers by December 2005 and 6 million and 740 million by 2010 respectively. In case of internet subscribers, the actual coverage has been well above the targeted coverage and has been achieved much earlier. By the quarter ending June, 2004 the number of Internet subscribers reached 4.93 million. This growth has been facilitated due to zero licence fees.

The role of Ministry of ICT in supporting the development of information technology is really commendable. In this information/knowledge intensive world, communication holds the key. The intra-regional and inter-regional connectivity is a need of the hour if we want to grab the opportunities offered by globalisation. It is worth mentioning here that presently we are having sufficiently adequate telecom, ISP, and cellular networks within the country to connect its cities and towns. We are having reliable satellite and submarine communication links that facilitate good computer connectivity with the rest of the world. The companies engaged in IT outsourcing to India can be assured of connectivity.

---

10. F - all such information see Mehra, 2005: 23-24.

The draft of the New Telecom Policy, 2005-06 appears to be another step to ensure the quality of services in Telecom, as special attention has been paid to consumer issues. It calls for setting up the 'institution of ombudsman, for consumer grievances'. It is likely to push for faster spread of broadband, local content, affordable PCs, internet application and e-initiatives.

IT Boom Hits the Shores of India

As per NASSCOM, like the IT boom of the late 20th Century, the 21st century belongs to services. A NASSCOM–McKinsey study predicts that India's IT industry will be worth US$ 77 billion by 2008; it will employ four million people and account for 7 per cent of India's GDP and 30 per cent of India's foreign exchange inflows. In view of its potential, the IT sector has been regarded as one of the top five priority industries in India. Many initiatives have been introduced to develop and benefit the IT industry. These are as below:

a) 100 per cent foreign investment has been permitted in this sector.

b) IT units can be set up under schemes such as Electronics Hardware Technology Park (EHTP).

c) Export Processing zone and 100 per cent Export Oriented Units Schemes, which provide tax and other incentives such as duty free imports and corporate tax holiday for export income have been permitted up to March 31, 2009.

d) 'Served from India' scheme to accelerate growth in export of services has been adopted. Under this scheme individual service providers earning foreign exchange of at least Rs. 10 lakh would be eligible for a duty credit entitlement of 10 per cent of total foreign exchange earned by them.

e) An exclusive service export promotion council was to be set up as per Foreign Trade Policy, 2004-2009.

ITES-BPO—"Destination India"

ICT is the driving force of globalisation. The Indian ITES-BPO industry is a high potential and high growth segment within the country's ICT industry accounting for around 60 per cent of ICT revenues in 2004-05. It may be noted that business practices, theories and work timings have undergone drastic changes in the industry due to ICT driven globalisation. The emergence of new technology is gradually resulting in the removal of geographical barriers, accessibility of data with the click of a key and availability of information at low cost due to the disappearance of distance (thanks to internet services). The globe is becoming like a family and the work pattern and work culture are undergoing rapid changes. These days two buzz words for the firms are: business development and customer care.

For business development, ITES-BPO segment provides a major opportunity to firms. BPO came into India in the form of medical transcription in the early to mid-1990s. But now India is the world leader in global outsourcing with over 80 per cent of its control over the market. As on March, 2005, there were around 410 ITES–BPO players in India up from 285 in 2003-04. WNS is the front-runner followed by Wipro BPO Solutions and HCL Technologies BPO services. ITES-BPO is attracting both global IT and non-IT joints. The Indian ITES-BPO is registering record growth rate often in excess of 50 per cent. In 2004-05 the Compound Annual Growth Rate (CAGR) of 56.4 per cent was recorded by this industry, higher than any other industry segment in India. In the initial years of IT boom, 'body shopping'[11] was popular but it is predicted now that India will be a 'back office to the world'.[12] This segment has been amongst the largest employment generator and high revenue generator segments within the country (as is evident from Table 3.10).

According to NASSCOM-McKinsey estimates, this industry would create jobs for over one million professionals by 2008-09. In terms of job creation, the ITES-BPO industry is growing at over 50 per cent. Within the country, these firms are penetrating Tier-II cities such as Mysore, Nasik, Vizag, Chandigarh, Indore, Kochi, Shimla and Trivandrum. This will contribute to employment generation on the one hand and help removing regional disparities, on the other. Further, new work culture would be spread to these cities.

11. Thomas, 2005: 127.

12. *The Economist* (2001).

Table 3.10

Exports and Employment of ITES-BPO Industry in India

Year	*ITES-BPO Exports ($ Billion)*	*Employment (No. of People)*
2002-03	2.5	171,000
2003-04	3.6	245,000
2004-05	5.2	348,000
2005-06E	7.3	470,000

Source: NASSCOM.

It is important to mention here that along with other factors it is because of the commendable growth of services especially new services that overall health of our economy has been improving. This positive trend is expected to continue in future. As per Goldman Sachs' *BRIC Report*, India would be the third largest economy in the world by 2032. *AT Kearney survey* sees India to be the world's most favoured destination for FDI along with China challenging the US. Presently, India is the third most attractive FDI destination in the world, enjoying the highest ranking ever.[13]

It is important to mention here that, "India's sustained leadership over other competing offshore destinations is driven by strong fundamentals comprising a large and growing pool of qualified, English speaking manpower; keen focus on defining and adhering to global quality standards, the demonstrated emphasis on information security practices, the improving quality of telecommunication infrastructure with its cost approaching globally competitive levels and strong government support-focus on improving basic infrastructure and developing policies and an effective regulatory regime that favour the growth of industry" (Karnik, 2005).

It is this segment of the service sector which has brought in long-term careers for our young Indians. Recent announcements of NASSCOM to launch The NASSCOM Assesssment of Competence test (NAC)[14] and announcement of Call Centre Association of India and CII to launch a programme named 'eKaliber'[15] would help addressing the

13. Mehra, 2005: 23.

14. Anonymous, 2005c: 26.

15. Anand, 2005: 1 & 5.

two problems *viz.* generation of large pool of resources to meet rising demand and checking of high attrition rates respectively. In fact these measures if successful can help our present generation to leapfrog onto a new path of success and growth in their hay days and that too so early in life. Not only this, with a phenomenal increase of employment in IT, BPO, etc. over the span of just four-five years, it can be hoped that this primary employment generation will also have a trickle-down effect in that the newly employed skilled workers will create lots of secondary employment for semi-skilled and unskilled workers. This would to an extent help in the solution of the equity and unemployment problems of the country.

But the sustainability of impressive growth of IT and ITES especially has been questioned in the wake of some challenges in the form of rising labour costs, rapid growth in demand for talented manpower/quality staff (shortage of workforce in BPO industry is likely to be 2,62,000 employees by 2009), high attrition rate (average attrition rate estimated at 55 per cent), outsourcing backlash, etc. Limited career opportunities, early stagnation, late promotions and lack of long-term options are other challenges in the BPO segment.

IT and ITES: The Flip Side

The growth of IT/ITES segment of services sector too has economic (inequalities-social distress), social (health, marriages) and ethical dimensions.

There is no doubt about the fact that the jobs available in IT and ITES are very promising from the point of view of salaries. In a buoyant Indian economy, almost every sub-sector within broad services sector, from organised retail to IT and ITES, is scrambling for manpower. But the services jobs especially in call centres imply a host of insecurities and vulnerabilities which get reflected in high attrition rates despite big pay packets. The studies reveal that the expiry of contractual term, increased stress and lack of career prospects within the firm are amongst the push factors. The jobs in BPO are quite demanding. The close monitoring, continuous work assessments, less number of holidays, absence of organisational activities and promotion of individualisation leads to isolation on the one hand and reduces the scope for establishing trade unions on the other.[16]

It has also been pointed out that "the attraction of high salary/ perks in BPO also gets murky when it is juxtaposed with the education and opportunity cost of the employees. As majority of them are educated in expensive institutions, the average cost of their education far exceeds that of an ordinary Indian graduate. Thus, these agents represent a group of expensively educated cheap labour. The long-term opportunity cost of BPO workers could be still higher. Most of these youngsters are in fact burning out their formative years as 'cyber-coolies', the toll of which is very high" (Ramesh, 2004: 496). Further, entering BPO sector after graduation means break in studies. The low-end nature of work (done by receptionists or computer operators earlier) in case of most of the employees means little scope for skill upgradation except picking up accents or communication skills. In fact gaining specific accents may adversely affect the future job prospect of the employees.[17]

Another shocking reality of such growth of services sector has resulted in perpetuating inequalities and disparities. The wage disparities have widened the social disparities and economic inequalities. On the one side we are having sky scrappers, posh colonies but on the other, slums clusters and people living on foot paths. On the one hand we are having CEOs who are getting paid exorbitantly and, on the other, are casual and other workers who get meager wages. The difference is well reflected in the words of Madapati (2005), who says that "Since 1980, the average pay of regular working people increased just 66 per cent, while CEO pay grew a whopping 1,996 per cent. According to *Business Week*, the average CEO of major corporations made 42 times the average hourly worker's pay in 1980, 85 times in 1990 and a staggering 531 times in 2000." Though there are several lectures, seminars, conferences held on good governance so that benefits of growth could percolate downwards yet the fact of the matter is that the performance of state has been quite dismal in checking and controlling inequitable process.

16. Ramesh, 2004: 496.

17. ibid.

Coming now to the gender aspect of work, though call centres and jobs are looked upon as 'women-centric' jobs, yet the atypical work timings act as constraint for the married women to take up such jobs due to dual responsibilities of home and work and also due to their reproductive role. That is why empirical studies reveal that most of the women working in call centres are in the age group of 18-30. They prefer to stay unmarried as they want to be economically independent and they find it difficult to balance their work with family life because of unusual hours of work. Some of the married women too enter these non-traditional employment sectors and supplement their family's income. But the traditional attitudes of males towards domestic roles and caring and rearing of children have not changed much. A woman's career is still considered to be secondary to that of man. The traditional household jobs combined with stressful nature of salaried jobs leaves them burdened. A redressal is due now. Otherwise inability to cope with stresses can have adverse psycho-social health consequences for women. Further, this is likely to affect the pattern of marriage, birth rates and marital stability in the years to come. A glimpse of that we are already getting after more than a decade of globalisation. There is a need that the role assigned to each sex must be made more compatible with that of men as well as women accepting their dual function of work and family.[18]

One cannot ignore the big question of safety of women working in call centres and other MNCs with shift duties. The recent incidents of the rape and murder of a woman call centre employee in Bangalore and an acid attack on another BPO employee at Pune triggered a debate on the safety and security of women employees in the BPO industry. Studies point towards the 'firewalls' solution for women working round the clock in corporate undertakings on the same lines as was given in case of data security phenomenon. BPO industry attracted lots of media attention for all wrong reasons. Data theft and fraud by some Indian call centre employees re-emphasised on the need to check malpractices of this kind.[19]

---

18. Based on Ramesh, 2004; Singh and Pandey, 2005 and Joshi, 2006.

19. Chebolu, 2006: 8-9.

Nobody would disagree that nothing is more important than the health of a person. But the kind of jobs available in the services sector especially in BPO (call centres) are proving to be a health hazard. A study reports that though call centres are most sought after places for young, fresh graduates and undergraduates as it provides them attractive perks (despite low skills and low level of qualification), transport facility, meals and refreshments and good environment, yet these jobs have adverse effects on the health of the employees as the biological clocks get disturbed. It is rightly noted that "...when energy levels are low, people are working and when the body system has high energy they are required to sleep. This adjustment process is not acceptable and the physical balance and well being of workers is thrown out of gear." Empirical studies reveal that the common problems faced by the staff of these call centres are stomach and sleep disorder, eye and head strain, backache and spondylitis, etc. They also get addicted to smoking and having endless cups of tea and coffee to stay awake at night.[20]

The nature of jobs which became available after new economic reforms of 1991 has brought about significant change in the lifestyles of our working population too. There is no denial of the fact that the professionals in services sector whether telecom or IT are well paid. But huge pay packets with prolonged working hours, reduced leisure time, sedentary life styles, stressful jobs have exposed our younger lot to health hazards in their hay days. With the opening up of economy in 1991 and a inflow of a wide range of consumer goods and plethora of international brands have brought in a new wave of consumerism in our country. The new consumer culture of jams, colas, wafers, ice-creams, pizzas, burgers is being experienced by our new generation. The mushrooming of fast food joints, pizza corners, coffee shops, shopping malls etc. point towards the change in tastes and consumption patterns of consumers. But this new culture has changed eating and drinking habits of a large proportion of our population. The intake of high calorie and high fat diet accompanied by sedentary lifestyles has been accounting for increasing cases of obesity and other life style diseases. Traditionally, a large number of deaths at a young

20. Singh, Preeti and Pandey, 2005: 684-88.

age used to take place because of infectious diseases, but now a strikingly different pattern is emerging. The pattern has changed from infectious to life style diseases like cardio vascular diseases, stroke, heart attacks, diabetes. The increasing cases of diabetes, heart attacks, backaches, spondalities, eye problems, headache and pressure because of the head sets and constant calls, earache, leg cramps, stress, depression and obesity provide an eloquent testimony to this fact.[21]

As was pointed out above, on the one side are those who are exorbitantly spending on luxurious consumer durables, but on the other are those who cannot purchase them. This would add to social tensions and would affect the pattern of production from wage goods to luxurious items which are consumed by upper middle class and high income group. It has been rightly observed that, "the damage caused to productive power of the country as a result of this frustration should be properly imputed" (Awasthi, 2006). There is a need to pay special attention to these socio-economic issues otherwise this would affect peace and stability of the country. Increasing crime rates, disturbing law and order conditions in several metros point towards this.

There is an ethical dimension as well to growth of services. Our young generation has got exposed to new culture through media as well as with the entry of new multinational giants after 1991. Recent online survey conducted for *India Today* by *MonsterIndia* (Feb 27, 2006) reveals that the onset of new global culture, more women joining the workforce, longer hours in proximity, a more open and intense environment have had an impact on office relationships, and cubical crush is putting strain on managing work and life after work. Of the 6559 respondents polled, a high 35 per cent (or 2321) admitted to currently having or being open to an office romance. Fifty-one per cent of those open to romance were married executives. This changed work culture and changed relationships can affect marital stability and give rise to vices in the society, on the one hand, and reduce productivity on the other.

Conclusions

Overall, we notice, to begin with, that the analysis of tertiary sector

---

21. *Business World*. February 20, 2006. pp.4-26.

has suffered from definitional and classificatory problems. Unfortunately, no single, precise and unanimously accepted definition of this sector has emerged so far. The ambiguity concerning the concept of tertiary sector prevails due to lack of universally accepted theoretical framework for defining services.

A review of the definitions of the services sector shows that the scope of this sector is getting widened. It encompasses in addition to conventional services, many new services also. The ICTs-driven globalisation, WTO and GATS negotiations have provided an impetus to bring about this change. There has been taking place growing 'tertiarisation' of the economy because of 'ICT-isation' of various sectors. These new services are playing and can play a very crucial role in improving the overall health of Indian economy on growth front as well as the employment front. IMF Report (September, 2005) has projected that during 2006, the global economy would grow by just 4.3 per cent whereas the rate of growth of Indian economy would well exceed it. While the rate of growth of many developed economies like US is expected to slow down to 3.3 per cent and that of other developed economies like Germany, France, Italy, Spain and Japan to not more than 2 per cent, it is Indian economy which is expected to grow at 6.3 per cent. "The Sun indeed rises in the east" (Thakurta, 2006). The services boom that we have been currently experiencing in our country has played a very important role in changing the traditional perception of the country from a 'land of beggars', 'snake charmers' and 'cyber-coolies' of yesteryears to a 'land of knowledge workers'[22] and making India noticeable globally. Telecom and ITES-BPO revolutions have already hit the shores of India and have made the futurists very optimistic regarding its bright future and performance ahead. That optimism is well reflected in the following words of Mr. Kamal Nath, Minister of Commerce and Industry which were a part of his speech at World Economic Forum, "...The question for CEOs the world over is no longer 'should my company go to India?', but rather 'can my company afford not to be in India?'. On the tourism front, it is Incredible India, but on the economic front, it is clearly Opportunity India..." (Mehra, 2005: 24).

---

22. Thakurta, 2006: 110-113.

However, we cannot afford to ignore the flip side of this rosy picture. The sustainability of impressive growth of IT and ITES especially has been questioned in the wake of some challenges in the form of rising labour costs, rapid growth in demand for talented manpower/quality staff, high attrition rate, outsourcing backlash, etc. Besides limited career opportunities, early stagnation, late promotions and lack of long-term options are other challenges in the BPO segment. Not only this, sceptics opine that the very nature of jobs in this segment is such that these are monotonous, mechanical, stressful and disturb the biological clock and therefore, there is not enough appeal of such jobs. Further, the growth of of IT/ITES segment of services sector has adverse socioeconomic, health and ethical implications.

Therefore, the big question which has come to the forefront after over a decade of reforms is that the process which was initiated in June 1991 to improve the quality of life of masses has really benefited them or has proved to be a hoax keeping in view the rising cases of lifestyle diseases, rising cases of divorces, crime and disturbing law and order situation in several regions of the country. Are not we then losing more on health, ethical and the social fronts?

References

Anand, Navneet (2005). "School Get a BPO Call", The *Times of India*, November 26.

Anonymous (2004). "Service Tax Goes for All Exporters—Kamal Nath Aims to Double India's Share of Global Trade by 2009", *Busines Line*, September 10.

Anonymous (2005a). "NASSCOM Announces Ranking of Third Party ITES", *Yojana*, October.

———. (2005b). "NASSCOM: 10 million Services Sector Jobs by 2009", *Yojana*, October.

———. (2005c). "NASSCOM Test for BPO Aspirants", *Yojana*, October.

Awasthi, D.S. (2006). "Indian Economic Development: Globalisastion, Transformation, Equity, Crime and Economic Thinking", in Raj Kumar Sen (ed.), *Erosion of Equity and Social Justice in Indian Economic Development*.

Bhattacharya, B.B. and Arup Mitra (1997). "Changing Composition of Employment in Tertiary Sector: A Cross Country Analysis", *Economic and Political Weekly* 32(11): 529-534, March 15.

Clark, Colin (1939). "Australian Economic Progress Against a World Background", *The Joseph Fisher Lecture in Commerce*. Adelaide: Hassell Press.

———. (1940). *Conditions of Economic Progress*. First edition. London: Macmillan & Co. Ltd.

Chebolu, Radha Mohan (2006). "Women's Safety in BPOs: Some Thoughts", *Effective Executive*, March.

Deakin, B.M. and K.D. George (1965). "Productivity Trends in the Service Industries", *London and Cambridge Economic Bulletin* 53:1948-63. March.

Dowie, J.A. (1966). "Productivity Growth in Goods and Services: Australia, USA, UK", *The Economic Record*, December.

Fisher, A.G.B. (1939). "Production: Primary, Secondary and Tertiary", *Economic Record*, June.

Foote, Nelson. N. and Paul K. Hatt (1953). "Social Mobility and Economic Advancement", *American Economic Review* 43.

Fuchs, Victor (1968). *The Service Economy*. New York: National Bureau of Economic Research.

Gershuny, Jonathan and Ian Miles (1983). *The New Service Economy: The Transformation of Employment in Industrial Societies*. London: Frances Printer Publishers.

Giarini, Orio (1987). *The Emerging Service Economy*. Oxford: Peragamon Press.

Government of India (2005-06). *Economic Survey*. New Delhi: Ministry of Finnace.

Hill, T.P. (1977). "On Goods and Services", *Review of Income and Wealth* 4, December.

India Today (2006). "Cubical Crushes", *India Today*, Feburary 27.

Inman, Robert (1985). *Managing the Service Economy: Prospects and Problems*. London: Cambridge University Press.

International Monetary Fund (2005). *World Economic Outlook*, Washington, D.C.

Joshi, Seema (2004a). "Tertiary Sector-Driven Growth in India—Impact on Employment and Poverty", *Economic and Political Weekly* 39(37), Sept. 11-17.

———. (2004b). "Human Development and Tertiary Employment in Developing Countries", *Indian Journal of Labour Economics* 47(4), Oct.-Dec.

———. (2005a). "Structural Changes and Growth of Tertiary Sector: Issues and Implications", Paper Presented at a 2-Day National Seminar on *Costs and Distribution of Benefits of Planning in India: A Review and Search for Alternatives.* Jointly organised by National Committee for Celebration of Birth Centenary of Prof. D.R. Gadgil and Indian Political Economy Association. Feb. 26-27. Garh Basai, Rajasthan.

———. (2005b). "GATS, Indian Services Sector and Trade Potential in Health Services", in *International Conference on Services Management*. Conference Proceedings, Institute for International Management and Technology. Haryana, India.

———. (2006). "Tertiary Sector in Developing Economies—Its Nature and Relative growth", in V.N. Upadhyay *et al.* (eds.), *Productivity and Quality: A Multidisciplinary Perspective*. New Delhi: Tata McGraw Hill Publishers.

Karnik, Kiran (2005). "Indian ITES-BPO: Vision 2010", *Yojana*, October.

Katouzian, M.A. (1970). "The Development of the Service Sector: A New Approach", *Oxford Economic Papers*, New Series, Vol. 22 (3), November.

Kindleberger, C.P. and Bruce Herrick (1977). *Economic Development*, 3rd edition. Tokyo: Mc Graw Hill, Kogakusha Ltd.

Kuznets, Simon (1958). "Quantitative Aspects of the Economic Growth of Nations; III, Industrial Distribution of Income and Labour force by States, United States 1919-1921 to 1955", *Economic Development and Cultural Change*, July.

———. (1966). *Modern Economic Growth*, New Haven and London: Yale University Press.

Lenglle, Maurice (1966). *The Growing Importance of the Service Sector in Member Countries*. Paris: Organization for Economic Co-operation and Development.

Low, L. (2000). *Economics of Information Technology and the Media*. Singapore: Singapore University Press.

Madapati, Ravi (2005). "Do CEO Compensations Match their Performance?", in V. Ramani (ed.), *CEO Pay Packages in the Global Economy: Issues and Perspectives*. Hyderabad: The ICFAI University Press.

Mehra, Vevek (2005). "India: A Preferred Investment Destination", *Yojana*, October.

Ofer, Gur (1967). *The Service Industries in a Developing Economy—Israel as a Case Study*. New York: Praeger.

Singh, Preeti and Anu Pandey (2005). "Women in Call Centres", *Economic and Political Weekly*, Feburary 12.

Ramesh, Babu P. (2004). "'Cyber-Coolies' in BPO: Insecurities and Vulnerabilities of Non-Standadrd Work", *Economic and Political Weekly*, January 31.

Reserve Bank of India (2000). *Report on Currency and Finance*, 2000-01. Mumbai.

Sampson, Gary P. and Richard H. Snape (1985). "Identifying the Issues in Trade in Services", *World Economy*, 2, June.

Stigler, George J. (1956). *Trends in Employment in the Service Industries*, National Bureau of Economic Research. Princeton: Princeton University Press.

Thakurta, Paranjoy Guha (2006). "The Sun Now Rises in the East". New Delhi: *Swagat*, Media Transasia India Ltd., January.

Thomas, Jayan Jose (2005). "New Technologies for India's Development", in Kirit. S. Parikh and R. Radhakrishna (eds.), *India Development Report 2004-05*. New Delhi: Oxford University Press.

The Economist (2001). "Outsourcing to India: Back Office to the World", *The Economist*, May 5.

Thomas, J.J. (2005). "New Technologies for India's Development", in Kirit S. Parikh and R. Radhakrishna (eds.), *India Development Report*, 2004-05. New Delhi: Oxford University Press.

UNCTAD/WTO (1999). *Business Guide to General Agreement on Trade in Services*, International Trade Centre.

United Nations (1968). "International Standard Industrial Classification of All Economic Activities", *Statistical Papers, Series M*, No. 4, Rev. 2. Sales No. E, 68, XVII. 8. New York: Department of Economic and Social Affairs, Statistical Office.

Unni, Jeemol and Uma Rani (2000). "Globalisation, Information Technology Revolution and Services Sector in India", *Indian Journal of Labour Economics* 43(4).

Worton, David A. (1969). "The Service Industries in Canada, 1946-66", in V.R. Fuchs (ed.), *Production and Productivity in the Service Industries*. New York: NBER (in Press). *www.nasscom.org*.

4

Debate on the Growth of Services Sector

Introduction

The relatively faster growth of tertiary sector *vis-a-vis* other broad sectors of the economies (which emerges from our analysis in the preceding chapters) has given rise to much debate on the subject. In this section, we shall briefly review the chief arguments advanced by those who have expressed their unease over the growth of services *vis-a vis* those who argue that the growth of this sector has been in consonance with the growth requirements of the other sectors. These two contending view points can be referred to as: (i) The Excessive Tertiary Sector Growth Hypothesis, and (ii) The Adequate Tertiary Sector Growth Hypothesis, which are discussed in brief below.

The Excessive Tertiary Sector Growth Hypothesis

Before taking up the excessive tertiary sector growth hypothesis, it may be pointed out that some authors consider employment in the service sector as inferior to that in the material production sectors. We may briefly refer to such arguments, to start with.[1]

First of all, the proponents of this hypothesis feel that average wage level and employee benefits in a number of services industries are low especially in comparison to that in the manufacturing sector. Further, low paying jobs imply 'little prospect for advancement'.

Many economists, journalists, business and labour leaders and politicians have expressed their apprehension that a growing service sector means 'a shrinking middle-class'. They argue that manufacturing jobs that earlier absorbed a large proportion of the middle class are

---

1. The arguments given by many observers in the context of increasing share of tertiary sector employment in US economy have been summarised by Browne (1987).

vanishing and services jobs which are created in their place are mainly low-paying jobs which employ hamburger flippers, sales clerks and janitors. Therefore, they feel the shift to services means demolishing the middle class.[2]

Secondly, they argue that "part-time employment is more prevalent in the service sector than in most industries, and those who work part-time are less likely to qualify for pensions and other benefits or to be considered for advancement. Widespread part-time employment may also establish norms for compensation and advancement that affect those who work full time."[3]

Thirdly, it is commonly thought that the services sector is incapable of generating growth on its own and, therefore, is regarded as dependent on the growth of other sectors, particularly manufacturing. It is thought that "they (the workers employed in the tertiary sector) live off the rest of the economy rather than contributing to it." These attitudes are summed up in the popular description of services as "taking in each other's laundry."[4]

Besides female workforce participation rate is higher in services. Therefore, rapid growth of services also means 'feminisation of poverty' (Block and Walker, 1982; Smith, 1986, Urquhart, 1984; Petiti, 1986) and 'shrinking middle class' (Stanback *et al.*, 1981; Bluestone and Harison, 1982; Kirkland, 1985; Petiti, 1986)

In India's context, some (like Patil, 1989) express their fear that faster growth of services sector as a result of rapid computerisation poses a serious challenge to industry and business all over the world and also in India. Patil says that computerisation in industry and business e.g. accounting, travel booking, banking, insurance, rail ticketing, communication, hoteliering and so on has certainly pushed up the growth of services sector but considerably, the services sector does not really create any wealth though it assists the manufacturing sector in the creation of wealth. Further, he says that the service sector is more glamorous, that is why most of our brilliant engineers,

---

2. This view too has been expressed in the context of American economy. For this see, Kirkland Jr., 1985.
3. Browne *op. cit.*: 53.
4. Ibid.: 52.

scientists and technologists are attracted by its glamour. He wonders, therefore, whether the continuation of this trend will deprive manufacturing sector of the cream of our personnel and only mediocre talent will be left to manage the production activities at the grass roots levels. He says that industrial countries like the US and Europe have already realised this factor. Now they are seriously deliberating as to how to attract intelligent candidates to manage manufacturing sector.

Patil (1989), therefore, expresses his apprehension that due to the above—mentioned two factors *viz.*, rapid computerisation and greater attraction of service sector we are likely to denigrate the importance of manufacturing activities.

Coming now to differences between the tertiary sector in Developed Countries (DCs) and the developing countries, Ghosh (1991) points out the following as the main differences:

Firstly, in DCs the emergence of tertiary occupation is an outcome of high level of income in other sectors. But in developing countries scarcity of employment in other sectors leads to the expansion of the tertiary employment.

Secondly, in DCs, the distributive services in the tertiary occupations are high-income type and poverty-induced, whereas in developing countries these are low-income and poverty-induced.

Thirdly, tertiary occupations in DCs are highly capital intensive in nature but those in developing countries are highly labour intensive.

We may now take up the excessive tertiary sector growth hypothesis and its core arguments.

In their study relating to Indian economy Bhattacharya and Mitra (1990) argue that if the tertiary sector expands rapidly and the gap between the growth rates of tertiary sector and the commodity sectors widens, then it would have adverse implications for inflation and balance of payments. Bhattacharya and Mitra (B-M) argue that since services account for a small percentage (it being less than 20 per cent in case of the Indian economy during the 1980s) of aggregate consumer expenditure and since marginal propensity to consume for material consumer goods is observed to be high (for the Indian economy) therefore, with the growth of income there will be relatively more demand for material consumer goods. In the commodity sector, income generation takes place through the production of consumption and investment goods but in services sector no commodities are produced. Therefore, growth of services income would push up the demand for commodities while their supply remains unchanged (an argument which has also been advanced by Kabra, 1989). So if there is a wide disparity between growth of income in services and commodity sectors, the gap between demand and supply of consumer goods in the economy as a whole would further widen. This would either lead to inflation and/or higher import demand for consumer goods.

Further, according to B-M, in an open economy this higher demand for consumer goods can be met by higher imports. But in a relatively closed economy (as India was at the time they were writing on this subject) this domestic demand supply gap cannot be automatically bridged by foreign trade. The excess demand in the domestic economy leads to a pent up demand for imported goods resulting in smuggling and higher import intensity of the domestically produced consumer goods sector. The relatively faster growth of services, therefore, increases the import intensity of not only the producer goods but the consumer goods also.

Despite widespread economic growth in developing economies (as noticed in Chapter II) poverty remains a hard reality in many developing economies. The three basic needs of their masses are food, clothing and shelter. These are all material goods and the marginal propensity to consume (MPC) of the poor is very high. Conversely, the MPC of services of the poor is low and, therefore, the services constitute only a small percentage of their aggregate consumer expenditure. We noticed in Chapter II that services sector in most of these developing economies has been growing more rapidly than the broad commodity producing sector. The widening disparity between the growth of income in services and commodity sectors can have adverse implications for inflation, balance of payments, and income distribution in these economies, as the argument of B-M implies.

Mitra (1988) in his paper in *Social Scientist* has also participated in the debate on the implications of allegedly excessive growth of the service sector in the Indian economy.

Table 4.1

The Service Sector: Developed Versus Developing Countries

Country	*Year*	*Developed Economies*		*Country*	*Year*	*Developing Economies*	
		*Proportion of National Income Originating in the Services Sector**	*Proportion of Labour Force in the Services Sector***			*Proportion of National Income Originating in the Services Sector*	*Proportion of Labour Force in the Services Sector***
Austria	2001	65	64.6	Bolivia	2001	63	42.6
Czechoslovakia, Rep	2001	55	55.1	Costa Rica	2001	62	60.5
Denmark	2001	71	71.3	El Salvador	2001	60	54.5
Greece	2001	68	61.2	Honduras	2001	51	35.1
Netherlands	2001	70	73.6	Pakistan	2001	51	33.5

Source: *: Calculated from figures in World Bank. *World Development Report 2003*.
**: ILO. *Yearbook of Labour Statistics 2004* .

With the help of data relating to different countries of the world, Mitra shows that the rise in the proportion of national income originating in services was normally matched by a corresponding increase in the proportion of the working force engaged in this sector in different countries of the world. But in case of India he notices a contrasting picture. With the help of the data Mitra brings out the disproportionality between income growth in the services sector and absorption of working force in this sector. He argues that due to this disproportionality the burden of unemployment and under-employment in agriculture and industry intensifies. He expresses his apprehension in these words, "Should the rate of growth of material output fall short of the rate of growth of population as it might happen in some years... other things remaining the same, the outcome could be widespread social distress. If the modality of official resource–raising further adds to this distress, the system may simply break down" (Mitra, 1988).

In Table 4.1 above, we have shown the latest data on the proportion of GDP originating from services sector and the proportion of working force absorbed in this sector in selected developed and developing economies of the world. By comparing them, we obtain similar results as reached by Mitra above. In case of most of the developing economies we notice a disparity between income and employment generation in services sector as in most of these economies services sector contributed more to income and less to employment. If this disparity continues to widen in developing economies then (as Mitra says in the context of Indian economy) it might have unfavourable social implications for these economies.

Mitra, in fact, is more interested in bringing out the social distress which lack of employment generation by a sector commensurate with its contribution to GNP may cause. But his argument can also be construed as implicitly supporting the excessive tertiary sector growth hypothesis. It is implied in this argument that if in developing economies, due to a relatively high labour productivity in the tertiary sector, the sector's share in GNP is high but its share in employment of labour is low, then in such a situation, the sector's growth can be considered as excessive, or undesirable. Some economists hold the view that net domestic product (NDP) becomes a misleading indicator of economic progress of a poor country if the tertiary sector grows rapidly. Chandra (1982) holds such a view. To quote him, "I believe that for India and most other underdeveloped countries the NMP (net material product) is a much better indicator of material progress than NDP." According to Chandra, the most urgent needs of the masses of a poor country are food, clothing and shelter, which are all material goods. Further, capital goods required for the generation of productive capacity are also material goods. Consumption services do not play much of a direct role either in the maintenance of the population or in the rapid growth of the economy. It is from this consideration that the rapid growth of the tertiary sector in India and elsewhere is viewed as rather undesirable. This argument suggests that growth of Net Material Product (NMP) should be considered as a more meaningful index of economic progress of a less developed country.

Katouzian (1970) had argued that the rapid growth of public administration which is a major component of the tertiary sector in most developing economies is not always guided by concerns for economic progress. If this argument is accepted (as is argued by Datta, 1989), a part of the output relating to PA&D of tertiary sector may be considered as having made no contribution to the growth potential of the economy. Some economists go to the extent of calling the growth on account of revaluation of PA&D as 'spurious growth' (Acharya, 2003: 39).

There is another angle to this hypothesis, *viz.*, that the services sector growth will accentuate the already skewed income distribution in developing economies.[5] The reason is that tertiary products are in the nature of luxuries for which income elasticity of demand is more than unity. So, whenever income growth takes place in this particular sector, this is likely to increase the consumption of luxuries by the rich or high income groups who have the capacity to pay for them. As has been already observed, income generation in material goods sectors is relatively slow in most of the developing economies. But the marginal propensity to consume (MPC) for the material goods is quite high because in developing economies like India majority of the population is relatively poor, and food, clothing and shelter are their basic needs which are all met through material goods. If the income growth in the material goods sector is low as compared to the services sector, it implies that the production structure will be out of tune with the structure of demand of the poorer sections of the society. This would surely widen the already existing gap between the rich and the poor and would contribute to already unequal income distribution. The growth of public administration and defence (PA&D) as a major component of tertiary sector is taken as the barometre for judging the overall performance of the tertiary sector.

The foregoing hypothesis, therefore, amounts to arguing that a high growth of tertiary sector is undesirable and that it is no indicator of real development. Rather, it can have serious implications for social harmony and growth of the economy as a whole.

The Desirable or Adequate Tertiary Sector Growth Hypothesis

The views of protagonists of the desirable or adequate tertiary sector growth hypothesis may be summarised below. Just as in the preceding section, we may review the arguments relating to the desirability of tertiary sector growth and the question of its adequacy, separately in this section.

---

5. Mohanty and Raghvan, 1990.

First of all, take the question of desirability of the growth of the tertiary sector. Lynn. E. Browne in an article has explained that average wage level in service sector is low as compared to manufacturing sector because of sex differences. He considers the growth of this sector to be desirable on the following grounds:[6]

Firstly, services sector provides more job opportunities for women than manufacturing sector as barriers to female employment are less severe in the former sector as compared to the manufacturing sector.

Secondly, typical service establishments are relatively less capital-intensive or more labour-intensive in nature, thus being consonant with the resource endowment of the developing countries.

Thirdly, it is in this sector that more opportunities for self-fulfillment are available which are not there in case of many industries. For example, it has been seen that sometimes people choose to do social and religious work or in many cases take up teaching just with a view to help others and not for getting monetary rewards.

Besides, Browne makes a further point about the complementary nature of services producing sector and commodity producing sector. Since the growth of one sector is inextricably linked to developments in the other sector, therefore, services industry cannot be considered as merely the 'passive beneficiary'. He cites the example of interdependence of computer services and computer manufacturing industries and health and medical services industry and drug industries.

Finally, he warns those who have deplored the increasing share of services in employment against drawing conclusions in haste. He says that "the point is that many industries contribute (to economic progress) and, ultimately, economic success is measured by the ability of the economy to provide a rising standard of living, and not by the shares of employment in particular sectors."[7]

Some issues raised in this debate (and reviewed below) pertain primarily to Indian economy. Hashim (1991) regards the expansion of services as desirable for employment generation, for better efficiency of the system and better quality of life. He says that the experience of

6. See Browne *op. cit.*: 54 & 57.

7. ibid. p.57.

most of the developed countries show that services sector has grown more rapidly than the commodity producing sectors. In the latter sectors there is always a search for economising technology which is an outcome of precision and efficiency in conversion processes, which in turn is achieved by mechanisation and automation. This resource saving technology is a labour replacing technology to a large extent. This is true in case of most of material producing industries. This dilemma of high productivity, high production and reduced possibility of labour absorption in material producing sectors is resolved by absorption of labour in service sector. Hashim suggests that research, innovation and application of higher intelligence should be included in the broadly defined services sector. "Expansion of services of this nature as well as those services which provide the essential coordination and linkages in the performance of separated and segregated economic activities makes the system work more efficiently and at lower costs."[8] He further says that education, health care, extension work and research are all parts of services, and make a direct contribution to both quality of life and productivity.

Now, we come to the discussion of the hypothesis why in India and other developing economies, growth of tertiary sector is considered adequate and therefore desirable. Ahluwalia (1989) argues that services sector growth (in case of Indian economy) should cause no alarm and in fact explicit measures should be taken by the government to enhance its role keeping in view the needs of the economy to create a strong infrastructural base (like transport, communication and housing) as also providing shelter and employment for the people. In her own words, "rather than worrying about too much growth in the services sector, the government should be creating conditions for faster growth of transport, communication and housing" (Ahluwalia, 1989). In her opinion, the fast growing transport and communication sectors would help to meet the growing infrastructural needs of the economy, while the growth of housing will help to meet a basic need i.e. need of shelter of the population. She opines that the construction work carries large employment potential and that is why the stress should be laid on promotion of the housing sector without any further delay. Broadly speaking, she says that in the present phase of development

8. Hashim, 1991.

the services sector as a whole provides a tremendous scope for employment whereas the manufacturing sector with its preoccupations of modernisation and technological upgradation can provide only a limited solution to the unemployment problem in the economy.

Nagaraj (1991: 247-248) in a note, attempted to test the validity of the proposition regarding overgrowth of the tertiary sector made by Bhattacharya and Mitra in their article referred to earlier. The point of contention according to him is that "the tertiary sector has grown relatively faster than other sectors throughout the post–independence period of the Indian economy." Using NDP at factor cost data at 1980-1981 prices, Nagaraj compares the growth rate of the tertiary sector with that of primary and secondary sectors for the period 1950-51 to 1987-88, as shown in Table 4.2, below.

Table 4.2

Changing Sectoral Shares in NDP: 1950-51 to 1987-88

Sector	*1950-51*	*1966-67*	*1976-77*	*1987-88*	*Changes in shares as per cent of initial values 1950-51 to 1987-88*
Primary	58.3	45.5	42.8	34.0	-41.7
Secondary	15.1	22.3	22.9	26.3	74.2
Tertiary	26.6	32.2	34.3	39.7	49.2

Source: Nagaraj, 1991: 248.

With the help of figures given in Table 4.2, Nagaraj shows that the share of tertiary sector in NDP (39.7 per cent) in 1987-88 is not only higher than that of the secondary sector (26.3 per cent) but also that of the primary sector (34.0 per cent). However, it needs to be appreciated according to him that even in 1950-51 the tertiary sector's share in NDP was higher (26.6 per cent) than that of the secondary sector (15.1 per cent), though both of them had shares lower than that of primary sector (58.3 per cent). Moreover, percentage increase in the share of the tertiary sector between 1950-51 and 1987-88 is lower (49.2 per cent) than that of the secondary sector (74.2 per cent).

Nagaraj further points out that according to log-linear trend estimates (which gives constant growth rates), while the growth rate of the secondary sector is 5 per cent per annum during the 1950-51 to 1987-88 period, it is 4.6 per cent per annum for the tertiary sector during the same time period.

He further elaborates his thesis with the help of figures shown in Table 4.3. These figures bring out the improvement in the growth rate of the secondary sector (*vis-a-vis* tertiary sector).

Table 4.3

Growth Rate of NDP and Its Main Sectors: 1950-51 to 1987-88

Sector	*1950-51/ 1959-60*	*1960-61/ 1969-70*	*1970-71/ 1979-80*	*1980-81/ 1987-88*
Primary	2.6	1.4	1.6	1.9
Secondary	5.6	5.0	4.5	6.9
Tertiary	4.2	4.4	4.6	6.4
NDP	3.5	3.0	3.3	4.8

Source : Nagaraj, 1991: 248.

The data in the Table clearly shows that the growth rate of the secondary sector since 1980-81 is not only higher than its record during the previous three decades but also higher than that of the tertiary sector in the 1980s.

Thus, the statistical evidence of Nagaraj seems to clearly suggest that it is the secondary sector which had grown at a faster rate than the tertiary sector during the entire period of 38 years under consideration. While the growth rate of the secondary sector witnessed drastic slowing down (with considerable fluctuations) during the period 1965-66 to 1979-80, the tertiary sector has displayed a much steadier growth rate since 1950-51. Therefore, as a result of a higher initial share and steadier (though at a lower rate) growth, the tertiary setor had come to acquire a relatively higher share in NDP compared to the other two sectors by the end of the 1980s. Nagaraj argues that if it is accepted that the domestic product has expanded at a faster rate since 1980-81, then in this period the secondary sector has witnessed a higher growth rate than the tertiary sector and, therefore, the latter sector's growth cannot be considered as excessive.

Resuming the debate, Bhattacharya and Mitra (1991) dismissed Nagaraj's evidence of a relatively faster growth of secondary sector *vis-à-vis* tertiary sector during the entire period since 1950-51, and showed that the increase in the absolute share of the latter in NDP is higher than that of the former. To quote them "...the percentage point increase in the share of the tertiary sector in NDP (13.1) has been higher than that of the secondary sector (11.2) during the period 1950-1951 to 1987-88. Thus in this sense our contention that even for the period as a whole (i.e. 1950-51 to 1987-88) the tertiary sector has grown relatively faster seems to be justified."

Responding, in turn, to the foregoing contention of Bhattacharya and Mitra, Nagaraj (1991: 272) argues that in their statistical evidence, B-M made a conceptual error of equating increase in absolute share of a sector in the total with its growth rate. Secondly, he points out that their attempt at dismissing the evidence, which questioned the basis for their empirical exercise in the earlier article, appears to rest on a partial and incorrect reading of his comment. Moreover, B-M's estimate of a higher growth rate of tertiary sector *vis-à-vis* commodity sector is an arithmetical result of combining the relatively large, slow growing and highly fluctuating primary sector with secondary sector. Moreover, their evidence that the gap between the growth rates of tertiary and commodity sectors has been widening since 1980-81 is based on the time periods they have chosen. With a different time period chosen, the results are bound to differ. This is shown by Nagaraj with the help of figures reproduced in Table 4.4.

Figures in Table 4.4 given below illustrate a recomputation by R. Nagaraj of the sectoral growth rates for each decade since 1950-51. These figures show that increment in GRD (Col.6) in the 1980s over the 1970s (0.2) is the same as in the 1970s over the 1960s (also 0.2). Hence, he says that it cannot be said that the difference between the growth rates of tertiary and secondary sectors in the 1980s has increased as B-M claim. Moreover, B-M's evidence of an increasing difference between the growth rates of the tertiary sector *vis-à-vis* commodity sector is contingent on their periodisation of the time series.

Table 4.4

Sectoral Growth Rate of Real GDP, 1950-51 to 1989-90

	Secondary	*Tertiary*	*Commodity*	*GRD*	*ΔGRD*	*GDP*
(1)	(2)	(3)	(4)	(5)	(6)	(7)
1950-51 to 1959-60	6.2	4.1	3.5	0.6	-	3.7
1960- 61 to 1969-70	5.5	4.4	2.8	1.6	1.0	3.3
1970-71 to 1979-80	4.7	4.6	2.8	1.8	0.2	3.4
1980-81 to 1989-90	6.6	6.5	4.5	2.0	0.2	5.3
1990-91 to 1999-2000						
1950-51 to 1989-90	5.3	4.7	3.3	1.4	-	3.8

Note: GRD stands for Growth Rate Disparity i.e., tertiary growth rate minus commodity sector growth rate.

Source: Nagaraj, 1991.

Nagaraj (1991) has dismissed excess tertiary sector hypothesis particularly of B-M and has tried to show that the shares of the industrial sector grew faster than that of the tertiary sector. Sharma and Jayakumar (1995) concluded after reviewing this controversy that "...one should desist from reading too much from the analysis of growth rate differentials. It all depends upon the size of the sectors as to how big they are in relation to the total demand in the economy."

Taking all the developing economies into account, Sabolo (1975), also addressed himself to the question of the overgrowth or adequate growth of the tertiary sector in these countries. According to him, the point that there has been an overgrowth of tertiary sector in the developing countries really boils down to the contention that in developing economies a larger proportion of total working force happens to be engaged in this sector than in the secondary sector and that the expansion of services has occurred much earlier (i.e. prematurely) in this sector than in manufacturing and other secondary sector activities.

The growth of employment in the service industries of developing countries is commonly attributed to two factors *viz.*, population pressure and rural-urban migration. Sabolo, however, considers it to be a superficial explanation which holds true only in case of traditional or old services such as street vending and domestic services which are registering a decline with the rise in the level of economic development. As a matter of fact, the expansion of employment in tertiary sector as a whole is accounted for both by new services such as education and recreation and complementary services like transport and commerce. These two kinds of services are expanding rapidly and providing ample opportunities for employment in this sector as well as contributing to the overall growth of the economy.

He further argues that to a large extent, the rapid growth of service industries is due to an increase in demand of both final and intermediate consumers for the services in question. This is not purely a fall-out of demographic factors though they do exercise an indirect influence (through the demand for education and urbanisation, for example). He says that growth of service industries is an outcome of import or imitation of the consumption patterns (demonstration effect) of industrialised economies by developing economies. Therefore, the consumption of services in developing economies is 'Overdistended' in relation to the stage of development reached.

Sabolo points out that though there has been faster growth of service industries in the developing economies, yet it should not be construed that there is an overgrowth of employment in tertiary sector as a whole. The evidence in fact points to the existence of pockets of underemployment in the traditional services which account for a gradually declining share of services generally.

Sabolo further argues that, "...the number of persons employed in the tertiary sector might nevertheless seem to be excessive if the number had increased at the expense of labour productivity. This does not seem to have been the case, although the measurement and the concept of productivity are very far from perfect."

Thus, this part of the foregoing debate tends to show that the growth of tertiary sector is desirable *per se* and is not excessive from the developmental point of view.

Conclusion

In the present chapter, we have reviewed the debate on the question of undesirability and excessiveness *vis-à-vis* desirability and adequacy of the growth of tertiary sector in developing economies. At one end of the debate are those who argue that services jobs are relatively low-paying which implies 'little prospect for advancement' and 'shrinking middle class'. Besides some others express their apprehension that there has been an excessive growth of this sector which would have serious repercussion in terms of inflation, balance of payments problems and more skewed income distribution.

The supporters of the opposite hypothesis suggest that the growth of this sector has been not only adequate but also desirable. They express the desirability in terms of the growth for employment generation, better efficiency of the system, better quality of life and also for meeting the infrastructural needs of the economy.

Despite this controversy, it cannot be denied that services and commodity producing sectors are complementary to each other. Growth of services industry is inextricably linked to developments in manufacturing industry. In this sense, services do contribute to growth. At the same time, it should also be recognised that if other sectors of the economy are growing too slowly to absorb increases in the labour force, or are growing but do not create ample employment opportunities then the growth of the tertiary sector becomes desirable to combat unemployment. Thanks to increasing use of automation and capital-intensive technology in the secondary sector, it is the services sector which has to grow rapidly in order to create the needed employment opportunities. The growth of this sector would be considered excessive or undesirable if it grows at a very high rate but the commodity producing sectors stagnate. The last-mentioned situation would disturb the balance between services and material production from the technical angle. Services and material production are interlinked through input-output relations and are, therefore, complementary to each other. Services such as transportation, communication, banking, insurance, etc. provide inputs to the material production sectors. Therefore, both have to grow in an internally consistent manner, so as to avoid shortages on one hand and surpluses on the other.

Besides this technical angle, the question of excessive and adequate tertiary growth can be viewed from the social angle as well. From the social point of view, it can be argued that since majority of the population in developing economies is poor, having food, clothing and shelter as its basic needs which are all material goods and since marginal propensity to consume material goods is quite high in these countries, the growth of services sector *vis-a-vis* material goods can become excessive. So whenever income increases, this would more likely lead to higher demand for material goods and their supply growing relatively slowly, this would lead to inflation and adverse balance of payments situation. Such a situation poses a threat to macroeconomic stability of the country which is judged with the help of such indicators as fiscal deficit, inflation and balance of payments deficit.

Thus, it is obvious that the growth of material producing sectors and tertiary sector should occur simultaneously because these two broad sectors are not competitive but complementary to each other.

References

Acharya, Shankar (2003). *India's Economy: Some Issues and Answers.* New Delhi: Academic Foundation.

Ahluwalia, I.J. (1989). "Services Sector: An Analysis", *The Economic Times,* January 11, p.8, Col. I.

Bhattacharya, B.B. and Arup Mitra (1990). "Excess Growth of Tertiary Sector in Indian Economy: Issues and Implications", *Economic and Political Weekly,* November 3, pp.2448-2449.

———. (1991). "Excess Growth of Tertiary Sector (Discussion)", *Economic and Political Weekly,* June 1-8, p.1423.

Block, W.E. and M.A. Walker (1982). *Discrimination, Affirmative Action and Equal Opportunities.* Vancouver: Fraser Institute.

Bluestone, B. and B. Harrison (1982). *The Deindustrialisation of America.* New York: Basic Books.

Browne, Lynn. E.(1987). "Services and Economic Progress: An Analysis", *Economic Impact.* pp.52-53.

Chandra, N.K. (1982). "Long-Term Stagnation in the Indian Economy, 1900-1975", *Economic and Political Weekly* 7, Annual Number, April, p.530.

Datta, Madhusudan (1989). "Tertiary Sector and Net Material Product: Indian Economy, 1950-51 to 1983-84", *Economic and Political Weekly,* September, 23.

Ghosh, B.N. (1991). "The Development of Tertiary Sector (Discussion)", *Economic and Political Weekly,* Feburary 23, p.452.

Hashim, A.R. (1991). "Forty Years of Indian Economy, Structure and Dimensions of Growth", *The Indian Economic Journal* 38, January-March, p.4-5.

Kabra, Kamal Nayan (1989). "Growth of the Service Sector and Inflationary Pressures", *The Indian Economic Journal,* October-December.

Katouzian, M.A. (1970). "The Development of the Service Sector: A New Approach", *Oxford Economic Papers,* New Series, Vol. 22(3): 362-382, November.

Kirkland. Jr., Richard I. (1985) "Are Service Jobs Good Jobs?", *Fortune III:* 20. June 10.

Mitra, Ashok (1988). "Disproportionality and the Service Sector: A Note", *Social Scientist,* April, p.5.

Mohanty, Deepak and V.S. Raghvan (1990). "New Series on National Accounts Statistics and Structure of Indian Economy", *Economic and Political Weekly,* July 7, p.1481.

Nagaraj, R. (1991). "Excess Growth of Tertiary Sector? Discussion", *Economic and Political Weekly,* February 2, p.247-248.

Patil, S.M. (1989). "Industry and Business: Four Challenges", *The Economic Times,* January 7, p.5.

Petiti, Pascal (1986). *Slow Growth and Service Economy.* London: Frances Printer.

Sabolo, Yves (1975). *Service Industries.* Geneva: International Labour Office. pp.3, 143-144.

Sharma, R.K. and Jayakumar (1995). "Structural Shifts and the Growth of Tertiary Sector in India", *Indian Journal of Labour Economics* 38(4).

Smith, J. (1986). "The Paradox of Women's Poverty: Wage-Earning Women and Economic Transformation", in C.C.Novak and M.H. Strober (ed.), *Women and Poverty*. Chicago: The University Chicago Press.

Stanback, T.M., P.J. Bearse, T.J. Noyelle and R.A. Karasek (1981). *Services: The New Economy*. New York: Allanheld and Osmun.

Urquhart, M. (1984). "The Employment Shift to Services: Where Did It Come From?", *Monthly Labour Review* 107.

5

Tertiary Sector Employment in Developing Countries

A Quantitative Analysis

Introduction

In chapters 2 and 3 we noticed that the tertiary sector in developing economies has been experiencing a relatively faster growth compared to the other two broad sectors and that the composition of tertiary sector has also been changing in these countries. In the immediately preceding chapter we took up the examination of two different and contradictory hypotheses relating to the faster growth of this sector, namely, the excessive and adequate tertiary sector growth hypotheses. Economic literature abounds with studies (Clark, 1960; Kuznets, 1966, 1969, 1972; Chenery and Syrquin, 1970) which reveal that there is a positive relationship between employment in tertiary sector and per capita income. But studies focussing on certain other variables which on, *a priori,* can be expected to influence tertiary sector employment in addition to per capita income are quite less in number. Both time series and cross-section data have been used for empirically verifying the relationship. Not only this, hitherto, research has been country-specific (Bank of Montreal, 1956; Kuznets, 1966; Fuchs, 1968) or specific to a country mix of developing and developed countries (Panchamukhi, 1986; Bhattacharya and Mitra, 1997). But studies relating to the determinants of tertiary sector employment in developing countries are few in number and the question has received far too inadequate attention from the researchers.

The main purpose of analysis in this chapter is to focus on the relationship between the percentage of labour force engaged in tertiary sector in developing countries and their gross national income per capita (GNIPC) along with certain other variables which have been incorporated in the studies conducted elsewhere. This has been done using cross-section data for various countries. A model has been specified to analyse the factors that are anticipated to influence the percentage of employment in the tertiary sector. The test procedure adaopted here is ordinary least squares (OLS). The sample is comprised of 24 observations. List of countries and data sources have been given in Appendix A.5.1. Most of the Tables have been prepared utilising data from various issues of *Yearbook of Labour Statistics* published by the International Labour Office. The organisation of the chapter is as follows: First, the model adopted here for analysis has been specified. Then follows the empirical results of the regression analysis, and finally the broad conslusions that emerge from this analysis as well as the policy implications.

The Model

The variables that are expected to influence the percentage of labour force employed in the tertiary sector (YTER) have been identified as follows:

1. Workforce Participation Rate (WFPR).
2. Trade Openness (TOP).
3. Percentage of Labour Force Employed in Agricultural Sector (YAGR).
4. Percentage of Labour Force Employed in Manufacturing Sector (YMAN).
5. Size of Population (POP).
6. Gross National Product Per Capita (GNIPC).
7. Degree of Urbanisation (URB).
8. Human Development Index (HDI).

The different empirical studies conducted on the subject established the following relationship between percentage of labour force engaged in tertiary sector and other variables.

The relationship between labour force participation rate and the percentage of labour force engaged in the tertiary sector is a controversial issue as pointed out by Nord (1989). As per Thompson and Black hypothesis (1975; 1976), there is an inverse relationship between the labour force participation rate and the percentage of labour force employed in the tertiary sector. But Warren and Gilory (1976), who were later on supported by Wheat (1977), refuted the above-mentioned Thompson-Black hypothesis on the ground that there was a positive relationship between workforce participation rate and percentage of labour force employed in the tertiary sector as this sector offers greater opportunities for women and teenage workers. The sign of the variable is, therefore, uncertain in view of the above controversy.

This variable has been included by Bhattacharya and Mitra (1997) in their article and measures the impact of globalisation on YTER. TOP represented by the ratio of the sum of exports and imports to GNP. It has been generally observed that increasing commercialisation and specialisation which is a concomitant of the opening up of economies, shifts labour from other sectors to the tertiary sector, particularly in the developing countries. Therefore, this variable is expected to yield a positive coefficient.

Our hypothesis in respect of the relationship among the growth of the three broad sectors is that the increase in employment in agriculture leads to decline in the employment in the tertiary sector and *vice versa*, while with the increase in the share of employment in the manufacturing sector, the share of employment in the tertiary sector also increases due to intersectoral linkages. The expected signs of the coefficients of these two variables are negative and positive, respectively.

As the size of population increases, the percentage share of labour force engaged in tertiary sector also increases because population pressures compel the surplus labour to shift to relatively labour-intensive and low productivity tertiary activities like trade, transport and a wide spectrum of personal services which have a potential for job opportunities (Mitra, 1992).

The inclusion of GNIPC is consistent with the works of structuralists' like Fisher, Clark, Kuznets and Syrquin. As per the structuralists' hypothesis, there is a positive relationship between the per capita income and the employment in the tertiary sector. Accordingly, the sign of the coefficient is expected to be positive.

The impact of urbanisation variable has been suggested by Duncan (1959), Stigler (1956) and Perloff *et al.* (1960). It was noticed by Clark (1940) also that there are certain services which can be carried out only in cities where the consuming population resides or at some centres where one can reach without much difficulty. Consequently, it is expected that as the process of urbanisation gathers momentum, the percentage of employment in the tertiary sector should also increase. This variable is expected to yield a positive coefficient.

Another variable has been included by Bhattacharya and Mitra (Mitra, 1997) in their article which measures the impact of socioeconomic development on the percentage of YTER. The variable is anticipated to have a positive coefficient.

Multiple Regression has been used to test the relationship between the dependent variable i.e. the percentage of YTER and other explanatory variables discussed above. The sample is comprised of 24 countries. The test procedure is OLS.

It is also important to find out as to whether there is any intercorrelation between variables we have taken here or not. In order to ascertain whether our analysis did, or did not suffer from the problems of collinearity or multicollinearity, the zero-order correlation coefficient matrix was prepared and studied. The data given in Table 5.1 shows that the problem of collinearity or multicollinearity does not exist in our following regression analysis. Even when we tried to test collinearity between variables, we found this problem to be non-existent.

Table 5.1

Zero Order Correlation Matrix

Variables	*YTER*	*WFPR*	*TOP*	*YAGR*	*YMAN*	*POP*	*GNIPC*	*URB*	*HDI*
YTER	1.0000	-0.4467	-0.2443	-0.6616	0.4897	-0.4325	0.4284	0.7765	0.5984
WFPR		1.0000	0.1994	0.3511	-0.1599	0.2869	0.1736	-0.0831	0.0428
TOP			1.0000	0.3149	0.3547	-0.1788	-0.0289	-0.2010	0.1767
YAGR				1.0000	-0.2704	0.4171	-0.3678	-0.4951	0.2608
YMAN					1.0000	-0.3722	0.3019	0.3506	0.4133
POP						1.0000	-0.2742	-0.2319	-0.4355
GNIPC							1.0000	0.6949	0.7354
URB								1.0000	0.6822
HDI									1.0000

Since the data are cross-sectional, involving heterogeneity of countries, *a priori* one would expect heteroscedasticity in the error variance. By applying White's heteroscedasticity test to the residuals obtained from regressions, it was found that R^2 was not significant and applying F-test, it was found that probability of accepting null hypothesis (Ho) stating there is no heteroscedasticity was high.

Empirical Results

Having hypothesised certain relations between the percentage of labour force engaged in the tertiary sector and the factors that influence it, we went on to test these hypotheses on the basis of the cross-section data for 24 countries, for the period varying between 1996 to 2000. We tried 16 alternative versions in this model and following were the results of different permutations and combinations. Each alternative equation starting from Eq.1 represents results which were obtained by running regression on the insignificant variables of the previous equation. In this sub-section we are going to present and discuss the results obtained from the regression analysis. The dependent and independent variables have already been defined in the preceding section.

In the first equation, when the percentage of YTER was regressed on the WFPR, TOP, the YAGR, the POP, GNIPC and the percentage of population in urban areas (URB), the value of R^2 turned out to be 81 per cent implying that on the whole 81 per cent of the movements in the dependent variable were explained by the independent variables. The partial regression coefficients of only two variables *viz.* URB and WFPR were stastically significant at 5 per cent and 10 per cent levels of probability respectively. It is clear from the Table that the regression coefficient on WFPR has negative sign. This is not in keeping with Warren-Gilory hypothesis of positive relationship between YTER and WFPR. The regression coefficients on YAGR and URB bear correct signs whereas that for TOP, POP and GNIPC yield incorrect negative signs. Elasticity estimates on the average value indicate that one per cent change in WFPR leads to 0.34 per cent change in YTER.

The negative signs of the regression coefficient of TOP may be due to the reason that the globalisation can have two kinds of implications:

positive (as hypothesised by B-M and given in an earlier section) that globalisation leads to increase in commercialisation and specialisation and thereby causes shift of labour force from the commodity producing sectors towards the services sector) and negative (as it may lead to closure of domestic industries if they fail to withstand the stiff competition posed by the foreign firms which often use more capital-intensive technology). So, this negative implication may be responsible for decline in employment in the tertiary sector with the increase in globalisation.

The negative sign of the regression coefficient of POP may be due to the reason that in terms of employment, the pace of structural change has been slow in these economies as most of these developing economies are having traditional structure (A-I-S or A-S-I) of employment. A large percentage of population in these countries is absorbed in the agricultural sector due to spillover of surplus labour force (a consequence of increase in the size of population) to this residual sector. Consequently, employment in the tertiary sector will decline.

The following may be the reasons for the inverse relationship between GNIPC and YTER.

a) The tertiary sector comprises low productivity services (informal sector) and high productivity services. In several developing countries, a large percentage of population is employed in the informal sector. It is quite possible that with the increase in GNI per capita, employment in the low productivity services (i.e. informal sector) may decline and thereby cause decline in overall tertiary sector employment.

b) Secondly, in the initial stages of development, as GNIPC increases, the share of commodity producing sectors in total employment declines, and that of tertiary sector increases rapidly. But the employment in this sector cannot increase monotonically beyond a certain limit because of the reason that a continuous decline of employment in the commodity producing sectors may cause stagnation in these sectors thereby leading to slowdown of employment growth in the tertiary sector as well due to intersectoral linkages.

c) Thirdly, most of the developing economies went for globalisation to promote competition, efficiency, higher quality of life and higher growth. However, the pursuit of growth objective (reflected in higher GNIPC/GNI) alone can have negative repercussions on employment. Although the tertiary sector is generally considered to be a relatively labour-intensive sector, yet it is possible that with the increase in computerisation and the development of information technology, this has become relatively capital-intensive in nature. Rapid computerisation in accounting, travel booking, banking, insurance, rail ticketing, communication, hoteliering, etc., means less demand for labour in these services. So, the rapid computerisation of services may be responsible for the inverse relationship between YTER and GNIPC.

In the equation 1(a), we have run the regression on those variables which turned out to be insignificant in Equation 1.

The variable YAGR turned out to be significant at 5 per cent level of probability and the variable GNIPC bears the positive sign as was expected. The value of R^2 turned out to be 51 per cent. The result shows that the impact of YAGR was captured by other variables in the equations. One per cent change in YAGR leads to 0.15 per cent change in YTER as indicated by elasticity results above.

When regressand YTER was regressed on TOP, YAGR, POP, GNIPC and URB dropping WFPR (Eq. 2), the value of R^2 dropped to 77 per cent. Two variables YAGR and URB turned out to be statistically significant and rest all other variables were insignificant indicating no change in YTER due to these variables. The partial regression coefficients on YAGR and URB bear the expected signs whereas on TOP, POP and GNIP care not in accordance with our expectations. The results given in the table further suggest that for a one per cent increase in proportion of population in urban areas, the employment in the tertiary sector increases by 55 per cent whereas one unit increase in TOP, YAGR and POP leads to decline in YTER by 210 per cent, 26 per cent and 5 per cent respectively. The elasticity estimates for the two significant variables (URB and YAGR) stood at 0.62 and 0.09 per cent respectively. When the regression was run on the insignificant variables of Equation 2, the variable POP turned out to be significant at 5 per cent level of probability implying that the effect of this variable was

Table 5.2

Regression Results for YTER, N=24

Equations	Intercept	WFPR	TOP	YAGR	YMAN	POP	GNIPC	URB	HDI	R^2	R^2
Eq.1	49.4703 (11.0769)	-0.2129*** (0.1122) ((0.34))	- 0.8003 (4.9919)	-0.2016 (0.1425)		-0.0363 (0.0307)	-0.0010 (0.0011)	0.5233 (0.1180)		0.8092	0.7419
Eq.1 (a)	63.6567 (6.5429)		- 5.3624 (7.4032)	- 0.4525** (0.2009) ((0.15)		-0.0492 (0.0446)	0.0014 (0.0012)			0.5120	0.4092
Eq.2	34.0877 (8.0678)		- 2.1888 (5.2819)	- 0.2658*** (0.1480) ((0.09))		-0.0527 (0.0315)	-0.0018 (0.0011)	0.5579** (0.1247) ((0.62))		0.7689	0.7047
Eq.2 (a)	59.3085 (6.8587)		- 12.5607 (7.3262)			-0.0944* (0.0436) ((0.09))	0.0022 (0.0013)			0.3817	0.2889
Eq.3	42.1615 (16.1405)	- 0.2520** (0.1035) ((0.40))	- 2.5094 (5.2271)	-0.2106 (0.1438)		-0.0201 (0.0322)		0.3698** (0.1296) ((0.41))	23.8934 (26.1770)	0.8095	0.7423
Eq.3 (a)	13.4927 (17.4636)		- 8.3984 (6.2208)	- 0.4317** (0.1618) ((0.15))		-0.0172 (0.0385)			73.6772** (22.7081) ((0.74))	0.6647	0.5941
Eq.4	25.7335 (16.5476)		- 4.7139 (5.8101)	- 0.2828*** (0.1588) ((0.10))		-0.0367 (0.0356)		0.3416** (0.1457) ((0.38))	23.6062 (29.5427)	0.7431	0.6718
Eq.4 (a)	4.5560 (19.5839)		- 15.887 5** (6.3428) ((0.16)))			-0.0611 (0.0397)			83.5200** (25.6024) ((0.84))	0.5391	0.4700

(Contd...)

(...contd...)

Equations	*Intercept*	*WFPR*	*TOP*	*YAGR*	*YMAN*	*POP*	*GNIPC*	*URB*	*HDI*	R^2	R^2
Eq.5	31.8680 (16.6906)	- 0.2465** (0.0996) ((0.39))	- 8.7994 (5.4197)		0.6740*** (0.3563) ((0.26))	-0.0304 (0.0288)		0.3764** (0.1201) ((0.42))	17.3613 (24.8333)	0.8228	0.7602
Eq.5 (a)	4.5560 (19.5839)		- 15.8875** (6.342 8) ((0.16))			-0.0611 (0.0397)			83.5200** (25.6024) ((0.84))	0.5391	0.4700
Eq.6	35.9952 (12.2357)	-0.2081*** (0.1064) ((0.33))	-7.5762 (5.0661)		0.6912*** (0.3539) ((0.27))	-0.0430 (0.0279)	-0.0009 (0.0011)	0.5003** (0.1141) ((0.56))		0.8258	0.7644
Eq.6 (a)	59.3085 (6.8587)		- 12.5607 (7.3262)			-0.0944** (0.0436) ((0.09))	0.0022 (0.0013)			0.3817	0.2889
Eq.7	17.8147 (8.5549)		- 10.5955*** (5.1896)		0.8326** (0.3726) ((0.32))	-0.0623** (0.0280) ((0.06))	-0.0017 (0.0011)	0.5343** (0.1213) ((0.59))		0.7867	0.7274
Eq.7 (a)	45.7861 (4.4924)						0.0030* (0.0014) ((0.15))			0.1835	0.1464
Eq.8	13.1921 (16.8719)		- 12.7249** (5.8734)		0.8462** (0.3960) ((0.33))	-0.0510 (0.0312)		0.3568** (0.1358) ((0.40))	!4.8447 (28.1219)	0.7590	0.6920
Eq.8 (a)	0.7873 (21.8407)					-0.4972 (0.0442)			76.3648 (28.4586)	0.3946	0.0.3369

Note: 1. Figures in the single parentheses are standard errors of the estimates and that in double parentheses are the elasticity estimates.

2. The data on YTER, YAGR, YMAN, WFPR, TOP and URB is in percentage terms and that on population and GNIPC is in millions and US dollars respectively. *=1 per cent level of significance **=5 per cent level of significance ***=10 per cent level of significance

captured by other variables in Eq. 2. R^2 turned out to be low at 38 per cent. GNIPC too bears correct positive sign in Eq. 2a. One per cent change in POP leads to 0.09 per cent change in YTER.

When the variables, WFPR and HDI were included and GNIPC dropped from the functional form of regression (Eq. 3), the value of R^2 improved to 81 per cent. The regression coefficient WFPR and URB emerged highly significant. The coefficients on rest all other variables were insignificant. The regression coefficients on YAGR, URB, HDI are as hypothesised whereas that on TOP and POP are contrary to our hypotheses. As per elasticity estimates, one per cent change in the two highly significant variables of the equation URB and WFPR led to 0.41 and 0.40 per cent change in YTER. When insignificant variables of Eq. 3 were further regressed in Eq. 3(a), two variables YAGR and HDI turned out to be stastically significant and value of R^2 was 66 per cent. The elasticity measured for the HDI stood at 0.74 which explains that one per cent increase in HDI leads to 0.74 per cent shift towards tertiary sector employment. However, the relative elasticity estimate of YAGR was low at 0.15 per cent.

In the regression Equation 4, we excluded WFPR and retained rest all other variables included in Equation 3. The exclusion of the variable reduced the value of R^2 to 74 per cent. But YAGR turned out to be significant at 10 per cent level of probability. URB was significant as was in Eq. 3 and one per cent increase in URB led to 0.38 per cent increase in YTER. When we run the regression on insignificant variables of Eq. 4 in the next equation, two otherwise insignificant variables of Eq. 4, *viz.* TOP and HDI emerged as significant at 5 per cent and 1 per cent level of probability in Equation 4(a). But R^2 dropped to 53 per cent. One per cent change in HDI alone led to 0.84 per cent change in YTER.

In Equation 5, YTER was regressed on six explanatory variables *viz.*, WFPR, TOP, YMAN, POP, URB, HDI. The Table clearly shows that the introduction of YMAN (or exclusion of YAGR) increased the value of R^2 to 0.82 implying that the explanatory variables included in the equation jointly explained 82 per cent of total variation in the dependent variable. The partial regression coefficient on WFPR bears negative sign supporting Thompson-Black hypothesis of inverse relationship between YTER and WFPR. The coefficient on WFPR is statistically significant at 5 per cent level of probability. The partial correlation coefficients of URB and YMAN emerged as significant at 1 per cent and 10 per cent levels of probability. The signs of the slope coefficients on YMAN, URB and HDI are as hypothesised wheresas that on TOP and POP are not as expected. The elasticity estimates of WFPR, YMAN and URB stood at 0.39, 0.26 and 0.42 per cent respectively. The regression on insignificant variables of equation 5 reveals that the variables TOP and HDI turned out to be significant at 5 per cent and 1 per cent level of probability and value of R^2 turned out to be low at 54 per cent. The elasticity estimates for HDI is 0.84.

In Eq. 6, regression was run after dropping HDI and including GNIPC. The variables included in the equation jointly explained 0.83 per cent of variation in YTER. It can be observed that the regression coefficients on three variables URB, YMAN and WFPR are statistically significant at 1 per cent and 10 per cent levels of probability respectively and the coefficient on rest all other variables are insignificant indicating that these variables do not cause any change in the dependent variable. The elasticity estimates of URB, YMAN and WFPR were found to be 0.56, 0.27 and 0.33 per cent. The regression on insignificant variables of Eq. 6 shows that the variable POP became significant at 5 per cent level of probability. GNIPC is bearing correct positive sign even though value of R^2 has come down to 38 per cent. One per cent change in POP led to only 0.09 per cent change in YTER.

In Equation 7, we dropped WFPR and retained all other variables included in Equation 6. The exclusion of WFPR reduced the value of R^2 to 0.7867. Only in this equation four variables namely, URB (1 per cent), POP, YMAN (5 per cent) and TOP (10 per cent) turned out to be statistically significant. As per elasticity estimates, one per cent change in URB, YMAN and POP led to 0.59, 0.32 and 0.06 per cent change in YTER. When regression is run on the insignificant variable GNIPC of the previous equation (Eq. 7a), not only this variable bears the correct positive sign, supporting the structuralists' theory of economic development but also turns out to be significant at all the three levels of significance i.e. 1 per cent, 5 per cent and 10 per cent. But the noticeable fact is that the value of R^2 has come down from 0.7867 in the previous equation to 0.1835 in this equation. The elasticity estimate for GNIPC is 0.15 per cent.

In the last equation, we included HDI and excluded GNIPC as these two variables cannot be included simultaneously in a single equation because HDI is almost a proxy for GNIPC. With the introduction of HDI, the value of R^2 registered a decline to 75 per cent. The partial regression coefficients of three variables, TOP, YMAN, URB are statistically significant at 5 per cent level of probability. The elasticity estimates for URB and YMAN stood at 0.40 and 0.33. In the next equation, YTER was regressed on two insignificant variables *viz.*, POP, HDI of Eq. 8. The inclusion of these variables reduced the value of R^2 to 39 per cent. However, HDI turned out to be statistically significant at 5 per cent level of probability.

Conclusions and Policy Implications

In the foregoing regression analysis, the variables human development index (HDI), urbanisation (URB), workforce participation rate (WFPR), percentage of labour force engaged in manufacturing and agricultural sectors (YMAN, YAGR respectively), size of population (POP) and gross national income per capita (GNIPC) turned out to be significant in various equations. The elasticity estimates of these variables bring out the fact that HDI (with elasticity varying between 0.74 and 0.84 per cent) is the most important determinant of the percentage of labour force engaged in tertiary sector followed by URB, WFPR, YMAN, YAGR, GNIPC, TOP and POP respectively.

The high elasticity estimates found in case of HDI points towards the fact that human development of the country can prove to be instrumental for employment generation and labour absorption in the tertiary sector. Therefore, keeping in view the positive relationship between HDI and YTER and high employment elasticity of HDI, steps should be initiated by the governments of the developing countries to increase resource allocation for education and health sub-sectors of the social sector and ensure their proper utilisation so that the value of HDI can register an improvement and can further result in creation of employment especially for skilled labour force in the tertiary sector. This becomes all the more necessary as many of the developing countries have embarked upon the path of liberalisation and globalisation during the last two decades and the process has consequently opened up unprecedented opportunities in the form of service revolution, mobility of capital and low communication cost (due to the advent of internet services) to some of the developing countries like India which are endowed with cheap labour and are consequently having comparative cost advantage. However, these opportunities cannot be exploited unless and until strong infrastructure is built up by these countries through investment in education and health sub-sectors of the social sector.

Our analysis also highlights that URB causes relatively larger changes (with elasticity 0.38 to 0.62 per cent) in the magnitude of YTER as compared to YAGR (elasticity varying between 0.09 to 0.15 per cent. It indicates that if further employment is to be generated in tertiary sector, then the labour must shift from low productivity agriculture sector to high productivity tertiary sector. This will happen only when the governments of developing countries intensify the process of urbanisation by way of industrialisation, focussing on the development of physical infrastructure, provision of public utilities like electricity, safe drinking water etc. in the urban centres.

WFPR is the third important determinant of YTER. Elasticity estimates in case of this variable varied between 0.33 to 0.40 per cent. The four equations, in which this variable has been included, support Thompson-Black (1975) and Thompson (1977) hypothesis, with evidence demonstrating that WFPR reduces YTER, given other variables in the equation, indicating that the greater concentration of labour force in the low productivity service activities may lead to "the phenomenon of discouraged dropouts from the labour force because prolonged or persistent work in low productivity activities reflect mainly the bleak prospects of graduating to a high productivity job"[1] (Mitra, 1992).

---

1. The negative relationship between WFPR and YTER obtained by us lend support to Mitra's (1992) hypothesis made in his paper in the Indian context. His hypothesis runs as under. The negative relationship between WFPR and service sector employment may be because of the reason that tertiary sector comprises both low productivity (trade, transport, personal services) and high productivity (public administration & defence, banking, public transport) sub-sectors. So when tertiary sector expands, it can either lead to more employment generation in the former or latter segments of the tertiary sector. But since overall employment growth has been sluggish in the organised sector, therefore, there will be greater concentration of labour force in the low productivity service activities resulting in what he has termed as "the phenomenon of discouraged dropouts from the labour force because prolonged or persistent work in low productivity activities reflect mainly the bleak prospects of graduating to a high productivity job."

YMAN, the fourth important determinant of YTER, with its employment elasticity varying between 0.26 to 0.33 per cent, indicates that since manufacturing has become service-oriented, therefore, as employment would grow in the manufacturing sector, there will be concomitant growth of the service sector due to intersectoral linkages. Therefore, while formulating any policy for manufacturing sector its implications for service sector should also be taken care of.

References

Bank of Montreal (1956). *The Service Industries*. Montreal: Bank of Montreal.

Bhattacharya, B.B. and Arup Mitra (1997). "Changing Composition of Employment in Tertiary Sector: A Cross-Country Analysis", *Economic and Political Weekly* 32 (11): 529-534. March 15.

Clark, C. (1940). *The Conditions of Economic Progress*. London: Macmillian.

———. (1960). *The Conditions of Economic Progress*, 3rd Edition. London: Macmillian.

Chenery, H.B. and Moises Syrquin (1970). *Patterns of Development, 1950-1970*. Oxford: Oxford University Press.

Duncan, O.D. (1959). "Service Industry and the Urban Hierarchy", Papers and Proceedings, *Regional Science Association* 5: 105-120.

Fisher, A.G.B. (1935). "Economic Implications of Material Progress", *International Labour Review*, July, pp.5-18.

———. (1939). "Primary, Secondary and Tertiary Production", *Economic Record*, June, pp.24-38.

Fuchs, V.R. (1968). *The Service Economy*. New York: National Bureau of Economic Research.

Kuznets, Simon (1966). *Economic Growth and Structure*, Selected Essays. London: Heinemann Educational Books.

———. (1966). *Modern Economic Growth*. Calcutta: Oxford and IBH Publishing Co.

———. (1969). *Economic Growth and Structure*, Selected Essays. Calcutta: Oxford and IBH Publishing Co.

———. (1972). *Economic Growth of Nations, Total Output and Production Structure*. Cambridge: Harvard University Press.

Mitra, Arup (1992). "Rural-to-Urban Migration, Urban Workforce and Tertiary Sector Employment: Inter-Relationship", *Arth Vijnana* 34(2): 107-124, June.

Nord, Stephens (1989). "The Relationship among Labour Force Participation and Service Sector Employment and Underemployment", *Journal of Regional Science* 29(3): 407-421.

Panchamukhi, V.R., R.G. Nambiar and R. Mehta (1986). "Structural Change and Economic Growth in Developing Countries", *VIII World Economic Congress of the International Economic Association*, Theme 4, December.

This chapter originally appeared as an article in 2004. "Human Development and Tertiary Employment in Developing Countries", *Indian Journal of Labour Economics* 47(4): 721-730, Oct.-Dec.

Perloff, H.S., Jr. E.S. Dunn, E.E. Lampard and R.F. Muth (1960). *Regions, Resources and Economic Growth.* Baltimore: John Hopkins Press.

Stigler, G.J. (1956). *Trends in Employment in the Service Industries.* Princeton: Princeton University Press.

Thompson, G.R. (1977). "The Relationship between Labour Force Participation and Service Sector Employment: A Reply to Wheat and additional Results", *Journal of Regional Science* 17: 476-477.

Thompson, G.R. and H. Black (1975). "The Relationship between Labour Force Participation and Service Sector Employment", *Journal of Regional Science* 15(1): 61-65.

———. (1976). "The Relationship between Labour Force Participation and Service Sector Employment: A Reply to Warren and Gilory", *Journal of Regional Science* 16: 419-421.

Warren, R.S. and C.L. Gilory (1976). "The Relationship between Labour Force Participation and Service Sector Employment: A Re-formulation", *Journal of Regional Science* 16: 415-418.

Wheat, L.F. (1977). "The Relationship between Labour Force Participation and Service Sector Employment: Empirical Findings", *Journal of Regional Science* 17(3): 463-466.

Appendix A.5.1

A Total of 24 Countries Listed Below have been Included in Our Analysis

Africa	*America*	*Asia*
Algeria (2000)	Argentina (2000)	Bangladesh (1996)
Egypt (1999)	Bolivia (2000)	Indonesia (1999)
	Brazil (1999)	Malaysia (2000)
	Colombia (2000)	Pakistan (1998)
	Costa Rica (2000)	Philipines (1999)
	Ecuador (1998)	Sri Lanka (2000)
	El Salvador (1999)	Chile (2000)
	Honduras (1999)	
	Jamaica (1998)	
	Mexico (2000)	
	Panama (1999)	
	Paraguay (1999)	
	Peru (2000)	
	Uruguay (2000)	
	Venezuela (1997)	

The relationship between the variables has been formalised as below:

YTER = f (WFPR, TOP, YAGR, YMAN, POP, GNPPC, URB, HDI) giving the following model.

YTER =

$$b_0+b_1WFPR+b_2TOP+b_3YAGR+b_4YMAN+b_5POP+b_6GNPPC+b_7URB+b_8HDI$$

The following are the data sources of various variables:

YTER = Percentage of labour force employed in the services sector.

Source: International Labour Organisation, *Year book of Labour Statistics*, Various Issues.

WFPR = Workforce Participation Rate.

Source: ILO, *Year Book of Labour Statistics*, Various Issues.

TOP = Trade Openness.

Source: World Bank, *World Tables*.

YAGR = Percentage of Labour Force Employed in the Agriculture Sector.

Source: International Labour Organisation, *Year Book of Labour Statistcs*, Various Issues.

YMAN = Percentage of Labour Force Employed in the Manufacturing Sector.

Source: International Labour Organisation, *Year Book of Labour Statistcs*, Various Issues.

POP	=	Size of population.
Source:		Word Bank, *World Development Report, 2003*.
GNIPC	=	Gross National Income per capita.
Source:		World Bank, *World Development Report, 2003*.
URB	=	Percentage of population in the urban areas.
Source:		World Bank, *World Development Report, 2003*.
HDI	=	Human Development Index.
Source:		United Nations Development Programme, *Human Development Report, 2003*.

b_0 is the intercept term and all the b's are slope coefficients. We have worked out the estimated numerical values of these coefficients. For example, b1 gives the partial effect of WFPR on YTER holding other explanatory variables constant. Each slope coefficient gives the rate of change in the dependent variable for a unit change in the value of explanatory variables.

6

Tertiary Sector-Driven Growth in India and its Role in Employment Generation and Poverty Alleviation

Introduction

The preceding chapters have dealt with different aspects of growth of and structural change in the tertiary sector of the developing economies. In the present and the following chapters, we present some perspectives on the growth of this broad sector in India, which in the contemporary world is one of the leading developing economies in terms of growth rate and size of GDP. In the present chapter, we mainly focus on the tertiary sector-driven growth of the overall economy, and its role in the generation of employment as well as alleviation of poverty in the country.

Sectoral Composition of GDP Growth

The analysis of the sectoral composition of GDP and employment for the period 1950-2000 brings out the fact that during the process of economic development, as it has been observed across various countries by Kuznets (1966), there has been taking place a growing 'tertiarisation' of the structure of production and employment in India. During the process of economic growth over the years 1950-51 to 1999-2000, the Indian economy has experienced a change in production structure with a shift away from agriculture towards industry and tertiary sector. These changes in the composition of India's GDP are brought out by data given in Table 6.1 below. The share of agricultural sector in real GDP at 1993-94 prices declined from 55.53 per cent in the 1950s to 28.66 per cent in 1990s. The share of industry and services increased from 16 per cent to 27.12 per cent and 28.09 per cent to 44.22 per cent respectively during the same period. During the 1950s, it was the primary sector which was the dominant sector of the economy and accounted for the largest share in GDP. But the whole scenario changed subsequently, and especially in the 1980s. The service sector output increased at a rate of 6.63 per cent per annum in the period 1980-81 to 1989-90 (i.e. pre-reform period) compared with 7.71 per cent per annum in the period 1990-91 to 1999-2000 (i.e., post-reform period). The tertiary sector emerged as the major sector of the economy both in terms of growth rates as well as its share in GDP in the 1990s. It is to be noted here that while agriculture and manufacturing sectors have experienced phases of deceleration, stagnation and growth, the tertiary sector has shown a uniform growth trend during the period 1950-51 to 1999-2000. In fact the recent years' experience shows that, "the growth of services sector has imparted resilience to the economy, particularly in times of adverse agricultural shocks as also during cyclical downturns in industry" (RBI, 2000-01: III-38).

Table 6.1

Sectoral Composition of India's GDP (Average Shares) and Growth Rates

Period	*Primary Sector*		*Secondary Sector*		*Tertiary Sector*	
	Share in GDP (Per cent)	*Trend Growth Rate (Per annum)*	*Share in GDP (Per cent)*	*Trend Growth Rate (Per annum)*	*Share in GDP (Per cent)*	*Trend Growth Rate (Per annum)*
1950-51 to 1959-60	55.53	2.71	16.0	5.82	28.09	4.14
1960-61 to 1969-70	47.37	1.48	21.10	5.48	31.33	4.48
1970-71 to 1979-80	42.68	1.78	22.88	4.50	34.56	4.61
1980-81 to 1989-90 (Pre-Reform Period)	36.06	2.91	25.13	6.46	38.80	6.63
1990-91 to 1999-2000 (Post-Reform Period)	28.66	3.18	27.12	6.21	44.22	7.71

Source: Central Statistical Organisation. *National Accounts Statistics*, various issues.

Employment Scenario

Next, we take up the structural change in Indian economy in terms of changes in the composition of the workforce. The sectoral distribution of workforce in India during the period 1983 to 2000 as shown in Table 6.2 below, reveals that the structural changes in terms of employment have been slow in the country as the primary sector continued to absorb 60.4 per cent of the total workforce even in 1999-2000, followed by tertiary and industrial sectors (22.7 per cent and 16.8 per cent respectively). There has been disproportionate growth of tertiary sector, as its share in employment has been far less when compared to its contribution to GDP.

Table 6.2

Growth of Employment by Sectors in India

Industry	*Employed Workers (Millions)*			*Annual Growth Rates (Per cent)*	
	1983	*1993-94*	*1999-2000*	*1983-1994 (Pre-Reform Period)*	*1994-2000 (Post-Reform Period)*
Primary	208.99 (69)	245.16 (65.5)	239.83 (60.4)	1.60	-0.34
1. Agriculture				1.51	-0.34
2. Mining & Quarrying				4.16	-2.85
Secondary	41.66 (13.8).	55.53 (14.8)	66.91 (16.8)	2.90	3.14
3. Manufacturing				2.14	2.05
4. Electricity, Gas & Water Supply				4.50	-0.88
5. Construction				5.32	7.09
Tertiary	52.11 (17.2)	73.76 (19.7)	90.26 (22.7)	3.53	2.42
6. Trade				3.57	5.04
7. Transport, Storage & Communication				3.24	6.04
8. Financial Services				7.18	6.20
9. Community, Social & Personal Services				2.90	0.55
Total Employment	100.00	100.00	100.00	2.04	0.98

Source: Datt, 2002.

The above Table also shows that the primary and tertiary sectors witnessed deceleration in growth rates of employment during the post-liberalisation period (1994-2000). In case of the latter sector it was mainly due to the sharp deceleration in employment growth in the community, social and personal services to 0.55 per cent in the post-liberalisation period as against 2.90 per cent in the pre-liberalisation decade. However, the overall growth rate of secondary sector employment improved from 2.90 per cent in the pre-liberalisation decade to 3.14 per cent in the post-liberalisaion period because of the combined effect of manufacturing and construction sector's rapid growth rates (Datt, 2002).

Table 6.3

Shares of Different Sectors in Growth of Employment in India

(Million)

Sectors	*1983*	*1993-1994*	*1999-2000*	*Increase during (1983-1993)*	*Share in increase (%) (Pre-Reform Period)*	*Increase during 1994-2000*	*Share in Increase (%) (Post-Reform Period)*
Primary	208.99	245.16	239.83	36.17	50.5	-5.33	-23.6
Secondary	41.66	55.53	66.91	13.87	19.3	11.38	50.4
Tertiary	52.11	73.76	90.26	21.65	30.2	16.50	73.2
Total	302.76	374.45	397.00	71.69	100.00	22.55	100.00

Source: Same as given in Table 6.2.

Despite the disproportionate growth of services sector and deceleration in its growth as noticed above, Table 6.3 brings to our notice two patterns of employment generation. The first roughly pertains to pre-reform period. In this period, primary sector was the primary source of additional employment (50.5 per cent) followed by tertiary and secondary sectors (30.2 per cent and 19.3 per cent respectively). The second pattern which developed during the post-reform period shows that the tertiary sector accounted for 73.2 per cent of additional employment generated followed by the secondary sector (50.4 per cent). However, the fall in employment in case of the primary sector is clearly visible in the Table.[1]

1. Also see Datt (2002).

Table 6.4

Sectoral Employment Elasticities on Current Daily Status (CDS) Basis

Sector	*1983-84 to 1987-88 (Pre-Reform)*	*1993-94 to 1999-2000 (Post-Reform)*
Agriculture	0.87	0.01
Mining & Quarrying	1.25	-0.41
Manufacturing	0.59	0.33
Electricity, Gas and Water Supply	0.30	-0.52
Construction	2.81	0.82
Trade, Hotels and Restaurants	0.87	0.62
Transport, Storage and Communication	0.47	0.63
Finance, Insurance, Real Estate and Business Services	0.49	0.64
Community, Social and Personal Services	0.52	-0.25
All	0.62	0.16

Source: Planning Commission, 2002: 158.

Table 6.4 brings out a sharp drop in labour absorptive capacity of growth in the economy (employment elasticity of growth) during post-reform period, reflecting the phenomenon of jobless growth. With the exception of two sub-sectors of tertiary sector, *viz.*, transport, storage, communication and finance, insurance, real estate and business services sub-sectors, remaining all other sub-sectors exhibited a declining trend in employment elasticities and thereby overall elasticity of employment declined from 0.62 to 0.16.

It is our hunch that in the current scenario, when employment absorption capacity of agriculture has reached the saturation limit (as pointed out in *Report of the Task Force on Employment Opportunities*, 2001 also), employment growth in the high productivity industrial sector is sluggish partly because of recession and partly due to the use of capital-intensive technology; it is the tertiary sector alone which can prove to be instrumental in employment generation.

Role of Tertiary Sector in Employment Generation and Poverty Alleviation

Services sector comprises a wide spectrum of both low productivity activities (mainly in the informal sector like repair and maintenance services, transport, shoe-shine, cobblers, hawkers, personal services like hair dressers, washermen, etc.) and high productivity activities (mainly professional, legal, etc.) as well as new services like software, IT (internet), IT enabled services (like call centres, design, business process outsourcing), cellular phone services (telecommunication), ATMs, credit cards, etc. (financial services) as well. As has been revealed in the Report of Special Group on Employment Generation (2002) in 1999-2000 only 8.34 per cent of total labour force got employment in the organised sector and the remaining 91.66 per cent was absorbed in the unorganised sector. Besides, there is sufficient empirical evidence which indicates that a large segment of the informal sector workers are employed in tertiary activities. As Mitra's study (1994) showed, in around 70 per cent of the class I cities i.e., each with a population of 100,000 and above, tertiary activities accounted for more than 60 per cent of the informal sector. Further, Hemmer and Mannel (1989) and Sethuraman (1981) also found that 75 per cent of the informal sector was accounted for by tertiary activities. Therefore, steps should be taken by the government to develop the informal segment (especially that of tertiary sector) by adopting sector specific strategies because employment generation through informal sector is also the least-cost option (ILO, 1991). Besides, the development of rural and urban physical infrastructure (infrastructural services) can be another source of employment generation . Growth of labour- intensive activities like housing and shelter should be given a boost as this will help to not only bring manufacturing out of recession by increasing the demand for construction related material and creating employment but would also help to attain the goal of 'shelter for all'. The rapid growth of IT ensures better job prospects for India's educated youth. As per NASSCOM-McKinsey Report (1999), IT-enabled services alone would create 11 million jobs and would generate a revenue of US$ 17-18 billion by the year 2008. However, knowledge-intensive economy driven by IT requires educated and skilled people with high productive capacities to exploit the vast opportunities being offered to us by service revolution in the current era of globalisation. Therefore, poverty alleviation seems to be a distant dream without expansion of the social infrastructure (especially education and health services) because services growth/growth can only offer us opportunities but people must have the knowledge, skills, capacities and capabilities to seize those opportunities. All this points towards the importance of building up and improvement of social infrastructure. The growth of the social sector can prove to be instrumental in the generation of employment for skilled and educated workers on the one hand and for doctors, nurses, paramedical personnel on the other. The growth of other related services provided by private clinics and diagnostic centres, etc. would further create employment. Above all, this would also help in the attainment of the long cherished goals of universalisation of primary education and 'health for all' as have been declared in Sarva Shiksha Abhiyan and Alma-Ata Declaration (1978) respectively. The foregoing can indirectly help in poverty alleviation because direct employment of educated persons also percolates benefits to the poor through generation of secondary employment in the form of cooks, security personnel, housemaids, and so on. Of course, social sector development will also benefit the poorer sections of society.

Is Tertiary Sector-driven Growth Sustainable?

A question arises about the sustainability of a high economic growth driven by the isolated growth of the services sector in the long run. This is because of various demand constraints (no demand from the other two sectors) and supply constraints (input supply to the other sectors). Ex-President Abdul Kalam and Y.S. Rajan (1998: p.158) highlight the complementarity of the three sectors in the following words:

> A country like India cannot hope to build its future on the services sector alone though it can be and will be a major component of the economy. India cannot afford not to build its strengths in agriculture for reasons of food and nutritional security. Nor can it afford to ignore manufacturing strengths for reasons of economic and national security. Based on the strength of these two sectors, it can build a major economic infrastructure for the services sector and use it to generate great wealth and employment for her people.

They further argue that if the services sector is properly developed along with the other two important and basic sectors, then this can be considered to be a sector truly at the service of the people as this sector covering multiple sectors of technology and manufacture will be instrumental in employment generation and individual prosperity.

The above-mentioned authors expect that the existing strong complementarity amongst the three sectors is going to increase in the near future with the introduction of newer technologies necessitating skill upgradation in all three sectors which would further accelerate the growth of the services sector. For example, the agriculture sector might witness much more intense use of IT than what it is doing now, be it in the use of remote sensing through satellite for regular monitoring of crops and soil conditions or water resources, or for weather forecasts through satellites and ground borne systems, or in the use of modern communications to be in closer touch with old or new markets. Similarly in the industrial sector, the reorientation of the skills from lower to top level will become almost a necessity with the use of sensors, modern electronics and IT. According to them, "installation of IT systems for all these sectors, training persons at all levels and maintaining and improving their skills would be a major service industry" (ibid.: 159). Consequently, the growth of skilled and professional services would alleviate the acute problem of the educated unemployed.

In the context of poverty alleviation and employment generation, particularly for low-skill labour, the interdependent growth of all the three sectors should be emphasised so that the country could achieve a sustained 8 per cent rate of growth in real GDP as had been envisaged in the *Tenth Five-Year Plan* (Planning Commission, 2001). Once this happens, trickle-down will start operating, thus making growth an instrument of poverty alleviation and employment generation. This would happen, particularly in the services sector, through intersectoral linkages. For instance, when the IT sector, the telecom sector, the retail trade sector, the automobile sector, etc. grow and expand, in turn these directly create demand for skilled labour. But the latter would in turn employ more and more of drivers, car cleaners, domestic help, security personnel, and a host of other low skill workers. Such employment generation, which would help in poverty alleviation, will follow the growth of sectors employing high skill workers in the first place.

The same may also be expected to happen in the rural sector where the growth of high value crop production, particularly the commercial farm sector (horticulture, floriculture, herbiculture, agro-processing and so on), would create demand for low skill labour belonging to poor families. Incidentally, the demand for such high value crops would have been generated by the aforementioned newly spawned urban economic activities like the IT sector and so on. Our argument here visualises interdependence of activities in all the three sectors, whose vigorous growth would help in poverty removal and employment generation as well. However, poverty removal would require a vigorous growth of the social sector (primarily education and health, etc.) and poverty alleviation-focused intervention by the government.

Conclusions

The upshot of the entire discussion in this chapter is that the appropriate development strategy for overcoming the problems of unemployment and poverty alleviation would be the development of the tertiary sector alongwith commodity producing sectors, with the latter providing a boost to the former. Besides the simultaneous growth of these sectors, it becomes essential on part of the government to introduce certain direct measures to develop urban informal sector (to tackle urban poverty) without neglecting the rural sector (to deal with rural poverty) so as to solve the overall problems of poverty and unemployment among low-skill workers. In addition, diversification of agriculture, public investment in agriculture-related R&D, irrigation, watershed development in backward states, solving the problems of small scale units should be taken up on a large scale,[2] while the processes of liberalisation help in accelerating economic growth. However, it is important to point out here that the focus of

---

2. The *Task Force on Employment Opportunities*, under the chairmanship of Dr. Montek Singh Ahluwalia, submitted its report in July 2001. The *Special Group on Targeting Ten Million Employment Opportunities per year over the Tenth Plan*, under the chairmanship of Member, Planning Commission, Dr S.P. Gupta, came out with its findings and suggestions for employment generation in May 2002. The two reports, however, differ in their approach to tackle the problem of unemployment. The task force found job creation potential of agriculture to be minimal as was reflected in low employment elasticity of 0.10 assigned by it to this sector for the period 2000-2012. However, the special group attributed low growth in employment in agriculture to low priority being accorded to this sector in the reform process. The special group identified several labour intensive sectors carrying employment potential like agriculture and allied activities, rural non-farm activities, small and medium industries, some of the activities covered under tertiary sector like IT, tourism, communication, financial services and also some sub-sectors of social sector *viz.*, education, health and nutrition.

employment strategy should be to strengthen the growth-employment generation linkages by exploiting the intersectoral linkages.

In this era of globalisation, the interdependence of various sectors is going to increase further. In order to make the manufactured products internationally competitive, the use of quality service inputs (whether domestic or imported) is becoming a pre-requisite. For example, as the use of sophisticated technology and specialised formal skills increases in the industrial sector, the demand for producer services comprising various professional and legal services, architectural, engineering services, etc., would witness an upsurge correspondingly and would create employment for educated youth. Therefore, it becomes essential on the part of the government to introduce certain key reforms to deal with cyclical slow down in commodity producing sectors, especially industry. In this connection Acharya (2003: 40) quotes Aiyer who says that it necessarily means solving the multiple problems of "a continuing high fiscal deficit,...lack of labour reforms and continued reservation for small scale industries; poor infrastructure, in the case of power sector getting worse than ever; problems in agriculture; insufficient reform in the financial sector; uncompetitive manufacturing, plagued by high (customs) duties and real appreciation of the rupee after 1996; and worsening governance" (Aiyer, 2002: 4).

The foregoing argument seeks to suggest that though overall growth in this country should be the cumulative result of the growth of all the three broad sectors, it is the services sector which will continue to enable the country to attain 8 per cent plus GDP growth rate, and its vigorous growth will, through intersectoral linkages, generate momentum for creation of employment opportunities and help poverty alleviation.

This chapter originally appeared as a special article in 2004. "Tertiary Sector-Driven Growth in India—Impact on Employment and Poverty", *Economic and Political Weekly* 39(37): 4175-78. Sept. 11-17. We are grateful to the Editor of *Economic and Political Weekly* for granting permission for publishing it as a chapter in this book.

References

Abdul Kalam, A.P.J. and Y.S. Rajan (1998). *India 2020—A Vision for the New Millennium*. New Delhi: Penguin India.

Acharya, Shankar (2003). *India's Economy: Some Issues and Answers*. New Delhi: Academic Foundation.

Aiyer, Swaminathan, S. Anklesaria (2002). "Stuck in the 5-6 per cent Groove", *Economic Times*, August 7, p.4.

Central Statistical Organisation, *National Accounts Statistics*, Various Issues.

Datt, Ruddar (2002). "Economic Liberalisation and its Implications for Employment in India", in Ashok Mathur and P.S. Raikhy (eds.), *Economic Liberalisation and its Implications for Employment in India*. New Delhi: Deep and Deep Publications.

Hemmer, H. and C. Mannel (1989). "On the Economic Analysis of the Urban Informal Sector", *World Development* 17(10).

International Labour Organisation (1991). *The Urban Informal Sector in Africa in Retrospect and Prospect: An Annotated Bibliography*. Geneva.

———. (1992). *The Urban Informal Sector in Asia: An Annotated Bibliography*. Geneva.

Kuznets, Simon (1966). *Modern Economic Growth*. Calcutta: Oxford and IBH Publishing Co.

Mitra, Arup (1994). *Urbanisation, Slums, Informal Sector Employment and Poverty: An Exploratory Study*. Delhi: D.K. Pub. and Dist.

Planning Commission (2002). *Report of Special Group on Targetting Ten Million Employment Opportunities Per Year over Tenth Five Year Plan*, May.

———. (2001). *Report of Task Force on Employment Opportunities*.

Reserve Bank of India (2000-01). *Report on Currency and Finance*. p.III-38.

Sethuraman, S.V. (ed.). (1981). *Urban Informal Sector in Developing Countries*. Geneva: ILO.

7

The Main Drivers of Services Growth in India

Introduction

As is quite evident from the previous chapter the services sector is burgeoning in the Indian economy (see also Mitra, 2008 and Joshi, 2004). In 2005, the services sector accounted for 54 per cent share in GDP, and 23 per cent share in employment and grew at a rate of nine per cent per annum since the mid-1990s. This sector is estimated to have the potential for creating 40 million new jobs and generating $200 billion annual income by 2020 as per *An Approach to the 11th Five Year Plan*. With 11.1 per cent growth, the growth momentum has been maintained by this sector in 2006-07.The share of this sector in GDP further increased to 55.1 per cent in 2006-07. This sector accounted for 68.6 per cent of the overall average growth in GDP in the last five years between 2002-2003 and 2006-07 (*Economic Survey 2006-07*). Not only this, India became the 12th largest exporter of services in the world in the year 2005. Services exports (at $311 billion by 2012) are likely to overtake merchandise exports (estimated to attain the level of $305 billion by 2012) by 2012 as per the latest study of FICCI. Services exports are growing at 28 per cent annually and goods exports at 22 per cent annually for the last five-six years. The share of services in the country's total exports would rise to 50.4 per cent by 2012 as against 37.1 per cent at present. Its share in world wide services exports will mount to 6 per cent by 2012, three times from the current 2.3 per cent, as the same study predicts (*The Times of India*, April 6, 2007). Further, the services have become a promising source of revenue, as 99 services are under tax net in 2006-07 as against only 3 in 1994-95. The service tax revenue increased from Rs. 407 crores in 1994-95 to Rs. 23,055 crores in 2005-06. The faster growth of services has thus been directly as well as indirectly contributing to the growth of the economy (*The Economic Survey 2006-07*: 25-27). Indeed, 'India is shining' as a result of the growth of the services sector.

However, the question which arises is: what are the sources of services sector growth in India? The present chapter briefly points towards the main drivers of services sector growth in India. It highlights that the main sources of services growth in addition to increase in income, increasing urbanisation, growing middle class and 'demographic dividend' from increasing working age population (15-64 age group) are a wide array of unconventional services though the role of the conventional services cannot be underestimated.

Main Drivers of Services Sector Growth

The main drivers of services sector growth, in addition to increase in Indian disposable income[1] (changing consumption patterns,[2] increasing demand for life style products[3]), increasing urbanisation[4], large pool of middle class[5] and a large proportion of population in the country's working age group of (15-64)[6] are:

1. Competitive Edge of India in Providing professional services
2. IT and ITES "Destination India"
3. Organised Retail Business Revolution
4. Real Estate Boom

---

1. Indian disposable income in 2003 was US $556 per annum and expected to rise to $1150 per annum in 2015 as per Goldman Sachs BRICs Report.
2. Change in consumption pattern is well reflected from the Fast Moving Consumer goods sector (FMCGs). "whether it is branded and packaged food and beverages or personal care or household care products, it seems as if we live, eat and sleep the sector" (Naidu, 2007).
3. Some of the factors indicating increasing demand for life style products are the figures of annual sales of cars (including multi-utility vehicles) which rose by six times to 1.3 million in 2005-06 (See 'Achyarya, 2007), the number of mobiles increased to 200million in Feb, 2007, 50 per cent of mobile phones sales growth is accounted for by replacement sales, further, there is growing Black Berry Magic (See, *The Hindustan Times, 2007*).
4. As per 2001 Census, 27.8 per cent population was in urban areas.
5. 35 percent of India's population as against 10 per cent in 1990 as per Bhalla, 2007 as quoted in Acharya, 2007.
6. As per *Economic Survey* (2006-07), the proportion of population in the working age group (15-64) has steadily increased from 62.9 per cent in 2006 to 68.4 per cent in 2026.

5. Booming Tourism and Travel Services
6. Growing Banking and Insurance Services
7. Booming Entertainment Services

Let us explain the above-mentioned sources of services sector growth in brief.

Competitive Edge of India in providing Professional Services

India is having comparative advantage in providing a wide array of professional services like IT services, Custom Relation Management (CRM), health services, educational services, construction and engineering services, legal services and accountancy services, architectural and design services etc at cheaper rates. Thanks to IT revolution, the services boom that we have been currently experiencing in our country has played a very important role in changing the traditional perception of the country from as a 'land of beggars', 'snake charmers' and 'cyber -coolies' of yesteryears to a 'land of knowledge workers' and making India noticeable globally (See Joshi, 2006a: 332).

IT and ITES "Destination India"

ICTs are the driving force of globalisation. It is being seen as the new engine of growth. The surge in services during the last two decades has been attributed mainly to high productivity services such as IT services and ITES (like BPOs, KPOs, MBPO, LPOs, RPOs, ESO, HRO[7] etc.). At present, India exports software and services to nearly 95 per cent countries around the world. North America (US and Canada) accounts for 61 per cent of our software exports. It is heartening to note that in 1999-2000 more than a third of Fortune 500 companies outsourced their software requirements to India.

As per National Accounts Statistics (2006), IT and ITES accounted for 2.6 per cent of the GDP. "The IT and BPO industries can become major growth engines for India, as oil is for Saudi Arabia and electronics and engineering are for Taiwan. Saudi Arabia's oil exports

7. BPOs stands for Business Process Outsourcing, KPOs for Knowledge Process Outsourcing, MBPOs for Medical Business Process Outsourcing, LPOs for Legal Process Outsourcing, RPOs for Research Process Outsourcing, ESOs for Engineering Process Outsourcing, HROs for Human Resource Outsourcing.

accounted for 46 per cent of GDP in 2004; Taiwan's electronics and engineering exports accounted for 17 per cent of GDP in the same year. ...India's IT and BPO industries could account for 10-12 per cent of India's GDP by 2015" (NASSCOM, 2005: 80). A NASSCOM-McKinsey study predicts that India's IT industry will be worth US $77 billion by 2008; will employ four million people and account for 7 per cent of India's GDP and 30 per cent of India's foreign exchange inflows.

India's offshore IT and BPO industries hold the potential to create over 9 million jobs by 2010, 2.3 million direct jobs and 6.5 million indirect/induced jobs[8]. In a study conducted for NASSCOM by researcher CRISIL (and released on February 20, 2007), for one job created in IT and ITES, four jobs are spinned-off in the rest of the economy in supportive activities like transport, catering and security, which generates employment for semi-skilled and even unskilled workers. In 2005-06, the sector provided direct employment to 1.3 million people and indirect employment to 5.2 million people as per more than 1100-member-strong NASSCOM President. Further, "Consumption spending by IT professionals alone has created 2.49 million jobs while the companies created 2.1 million jobs through other operational expenses incurred. Capital expenditure has led to the creation of another 0.63 million jobs in the sector so far", said CRISIL Chief Economist and Executive Director Subir Gokarn (*The Hindustan Times*, 2007: 26).

India has emerged as a top destination for offshoring as per Global Services Location Index 2007. India's share in global offshore IT services (i.e., outsourced software services) is 65 per cent and global BPO (business process offshoring) industry is 46 per cent. This was made possible by unparalleled export performance with a CAGR of 28 per cent over a decade. There is a lot of scope for future expansion as only 10 per cent of the potentially addressable global IT/ITES market has so far been realised. The remaining 90 per cent (worth $300 billion) remains to be tapped as per *An Approach to the 11th Five Year Plan.*

---

8. The offshore IT, BPO can support 1.4 million construction site and related workers in 2010 by creating demand for real estate/space, 1.5-1.75 million retail employees in 2010 as an estimated 80-90 per cent of employees spending will be on food, recreation, clothing and foot ware, utilities, transport etc. and an estimated requirement for 6, 50,000-7,00,000 transport personnel by 2010 (NASSCOM, 2005: 84-85).

Organised Retail Business Revolution

In addition to IT and ITES revolution, we have been witnessing the "Great India retail revolution".

India has been called a nation of shopkeepers because of the huge number of retail enterprises in India. Their estimated number rose from 8.5 million in 1996 to 9.3 million in 2003, 12 million in 2003 and 15 million in mid 2005. India has been identified as the "topmost attractive destination" by A.T. Kearney from amongst the 30 emergent markets. The retail enterprises' contribution to the GDP is 14 per cent and share in employment is 7 per cent or 42 million jobs (only agriculture employs more). It is the largest component of the service sector. The retail industry is divided into the organised and unorganised sectors. Organised retail refers to businesses each employing more than 10 persons and comprises corporate-backed hypermarkets and retail chains. It accounts for just two per cent (now three per cent) of the trade and employs approximately five lakh persons. Contrary to it, the unorganised sector refers to traditional formats of low cost retailing such as the local *kirana* shops, owner manned general stores, *paan/bidi* shops, convenience stores, handcart and pavement vendors, and employs over four crore persons. 98 per cent (now 97 per cent) of retailing takes place in this segment. This is highly fragmented with about 11 million outlets operating in the country and only four per cent of them being larger than 500 sq. ft in size. This segment is highly labour intensive (Ramasubramanian, 2006 and also see Joshi, 2006b).

The retail sector is expecting a CAGR of 35 per cent over the next four years as a plethora of global giants from the US, EU and Australia are eyeing the almost untapped organised retail industry in India. India's vast middle class has made it even more attractive.

"India's retail war has just begun to play out". Sunil Mittal's Bharti signed a pact with the world's largest retailer, the $316 billion Wal Mart. As Watson, with over 7600 stores globally is preparing a game plan to enter India. Mukesh Ambani's Rs.25,000 crores investment plan with an expected turnover of $20 billion by 2010, Kumar Mangalam Birla's Rs.15,000 crores retail ambition, Tata's tie up with Australia based Woolsworth, Adi Godrej's talks with leading global retailers including

Carrefour and Tesco, point towards the fact that Indian companies and foreign retail bigwigs are eyeing a slice of the $7 billion organised retail business. According to Ernst and Young, India's organised retail business is expected to grow at 400 per cent a year and is projected to touch the $30 billion mark by 2010 (*The Financial Express:* 18). That is why companies are on a hiring spree to lure the best talent. The retail sector is expected to generate employment in excess of 20 lakh by 2010, of which 5-6 lakhs will be needed in the organised sector itself.

There is no doubt about the fact that with the mushrooming of shopping malls, multiplexes which will provide food, retail, and entertainment under one roof, the urban landscape will entirely change over the next few years and the proliferation of the mall culture across the country will lead to a spurt in realty demand. With limited space and the consequent rising cost of land in Tier I cities and due to availability of land and large pool of educated and skilled workforce in Tier II and Tier III cities, the latter category of cities have stared attracting investment in recent years. Further, front end retail plans cannot be successful without a strong backend network in the form of warehouses and cold storages which constitutes the backbone of organised retail in India. The backend operations are likely to offer huge business opportunities for real estate developers and would contribute to both employment generation and overall growth in the tier II and III cities. Real revolution will take place when the rural economies will stand transformed over a period of time.

Real Estate Boom

Real estate involves purchase and sale and development of land, residential and non-residential buildings (like commercial offices, trading spaces such as theatres, hotels and restaurants, retail outlets, traditional buildings such as factories and government buildings) (*Tenth Five Year Plan*: 829). After the onset of reforms, the real estate sector comprising of a collection of industrial and services sectors of the economy has assumed growing importance. The year 2006 saw a real estate boom which is likely to gather momentum in 2007. The boom is not solely the outcome of scarcity of land and regulations. The booming economy coupled with rapidly growing IT and ITES and organised retail sectors are driving the Indian real estate boom by pushing up the demand for commercial office space, and good quality housing units for their employees. The growing demand for space has pushed up the contribution of the real estate sector from 5 to 6 per cent of GDP. Realty is now the second largest employer after agriculture.

The sunrise sectors like IT and ITES, telecom, organised retail, hospitality and entertainment sector, financial services and emerging sectors such as, pharmaceuticals, bio-technology have provided a boost to the demand for realty especially commercial office space. Favourable demographics, urbanisation, increasing purchasing power, a large segment of population in the working age group, strong belief of the young group in "buy and pay" as opposed to "save and repay", ardent consumerism and easier access to finance are fuelling demand for residential accommodation. Further certain policy measures like 100 per cent FDI in the construction business from March 2005, provision for setting up of Software Technology Parks, Bio-Tech parks and Special Economic Zones (SEZs)[9] and greater integration with the global economy and forthcoming Common Wealth Games have also contributed to the increasing demand for realty.

"With stock markets being highly volatile, investment in real estate has begun to look attractive and competitive with typical yields being 20-25 per cent per annum", ASSOCHAM President Anil Agarwal said, adding that the sector would offer a good investment alternative to stocks in coming years.

Global players like Royal Indian Raj International, Blackstone, Goldman Sachs, Emmar properties, Citigroup property, Morgan Stanley etc. are trying to encash the boom in the realty segment.

Assocham feels that the sector, currently valued at $16 billion, is growing at a rate of 30 per cent compounded annual growth rate (CAGR). It forecasts that the realty sector would grow from 12 billion dollar to 90 billion dollar. According to Future of Real Estate investment in India, a study published by ASSOCHAM, the real estate share in expected FDI inflow of $8 billion in 2006-2007 would be about 26.5 per cent.

9. SEZs are emerging as new investment destinations for realty developers. Out of 250 SEZs approved so far, 85 are in the IT and ITES segment, 10-15 in the electronic area and 17 in manufacturing and engineering areas.

Booming Tourism and Travel Services

India is a unique country which can offer a variety of tourism services varying from natural, cultural, business, and leisure tourism to spiritual, religious, ecological, adventure and medical tourism. As has been rightly pointed out by the CII, "with yoga, meditation, ayurveda, allopathy, and other systems of medicine, India offers a unique basket of services to an individual that is difficult to match by other countries."

Growing foreign tourist arrival at the rate of 10 per cent, expectation of the arrival of 36 lakh foreign tourists in 2007, 100 per cent occupancy in hotels in the luxury and business traveller segment, sky high hotel tariffs, approval of 1,15,000 hotel rooms by the Ministry of Tourism around the country are indicative of booming tourism and hospitality segment of services sector in India (*India Today*, Jan 1, 2007).

According to The World Travel and Tourism Council's 2006 Travel and Tourism Economic Research, the Travel and tourism sector in India is expected to generate a total demand of US $53,544.5 millon of economic activity, accounting for 5.4 per cent of GDP and 5.4 per cent of total employment. The sector is expected to grow at a rate of 8.4 per cent in 2006 and 8 per cent per annum in real terms between 2007 and 2016. Tourism is the third largest net earner of forex. Forex earning from tourism stood at US $6 billion in 2005. The WTO has ranked India 5th among the world's tourist spots. The tourist arrival is expected to touch 10 million in 2011 and 15 million by 2014.

India's high GDP growth rate with relatively liberal policy regime with respect to private sector and foreign investment, along with policy initiatives like liberalisation in the aviation sector, open skies policy, rationalisation in tax rates in the hospitality sector, tourist friendly visa, immigration services, procedural changes in making available land for construction of hotels, allowing setting up of guest houses, identification of 31 villages for developing tourist hubs in different states and successful Incredible India campaign are behind the booming tourism and hospitality sector and getting India placed as number four among the world's must-see countries.[10]

---

10. The Readers Travel Awards, 2006, conducted by Conde Nast Traveller has recently placed India number four (up from number nine in 2003) among the world's must see destinations.

Growing Banking and Insurance Services

The banking sector is the most dominant segment of the financial system of India. It indicates not only the financial health of the country but also plays an important role in propelling the economic growth of the country by channelising resources to all the sectors of the economy. The banking sector with 222 commercial banks in India (of which 133 are Regional Rural Banks (RRBs)) operating with 68,681 branches (as in March 2006)[11] along with the Indian insurance market (2004-05) whose value is estimated at Rs. 450 billion (US$10 billion) accounts for 7 per cent to the country's GDP.

Retail banking is growing explosively (from a total value of Rs.495 bn in 2000 to Rs.2970 bn in 2005) and the insurance sector is growing at the rate of 15-20 per cent annually. Banks have been offering mass banking products and gradually shifting their focus from mass banking to class banking[12] with introduction of value added and customised products.

Deregulation of administered structure of interest rates,[13] equity participation by the private investors in Government owned banks[14], establishment of new banks in the private sector,[15] the relaxation of norms for the entry of foreign banks, and allowing of FDI up to 74 per cent in the private sector banks are some of the measures which have raised the efficiency and productivity of the banking sector. The

---

11. see *http://www.ficci.com/media room/speeches-presentation/2006/speeches-2006.htm.*

12. Mass banking products offered by banks are: a) Savings Bank, Current Account, Term deposit Account; b) Cash Credit, Term Loans; c) Issuance of Drafts, Telegraphic Transfers, Bankers Cheque and Internal Transfer of funds. Class banking implies the introduction of value added and customised products like: a) Investment Advisory Services, SGL II accounts, Photo-credit cards, Cash Management services, Investment products and Tax Advisory services; b) mutual fund schemes; c)Home banking has already become common; d) debit cards, flexi deposits, ATM cards, personal loans including consumer loans, housing loans and vehicle loans have been introduced by a number of banks; e)housing loans, car loans, personal loans, consumer durable loans, education loans, loans against share, financing against gold.

13. Except for savings deposit accounts, non-resident Indian (NRI) deposits, small loans up to Rs. two lakh

14. The share of the public sector banks in the aggregate assets of the banking sector has come down from 90 per cent in 1991 to around 75 per cent in 2004.

15. For this and the forgoing see *The Financial Express*, March 15, 2007.

banking industry has provided employment to nine lakh people currently, and is expected to create additional employment for six lakh people over the next five years.

"A well-developed and evolved insurance sector is needed for economic development as it provides long term funds for infrastructure development and at the same time strengthens the risk-taking ability. It is estimated that over the next 10 years India would require investments of the order of one trillion US dollars. The Insurance sector, to some extent, can enable investments in infrastructure development to sustain economic growth of the country" (*The Financial Express*, February, 2007).

So far as the insurance sector is concerned, there is enormous scope for expansion of this sector because of the increase in income, awareness about insurance products and the presence of a huge middle class which can afford to buy life, health and disability and pension plan products. The Insurance sector has been opened for competition and private participation has also been allowed through the enactment of the Insurance Regulatory and Development Authority Act, 1999 (IRDA Act). Further, to protect the interests of the insurance policy holders and to regulate, promote the orderly growth of the insurance industry, Insurance regulatory and Development Authority was set up on April 19, 2000. Insurance penetration (ratio of premium to GDP) has gone up from 1.93 per cent in 1999 to 3.28 per cent in 2003. But it is still low as compared to developed countries where it varies in the range of 7.0 per cent to 15 per cent. Penetration is especially low in non-life segment of Insurance services. There is less than 12 per cent of the workforce covered by any pension plan. Since the number of persons over 60 years is likely to rise from 90 million to 175 million in 2030, therefore, the non-life segment of insurance offers a huge market. There are a large number of life insurance policies in force in India. Though gross premium collection is nearly 2 per cent of GDP yet nearly 80 per cent of Indian population is without life insurance cover, indicating the immense untapped potential of this sector. The entry of private players (24 foreign players and more than 15 in the pipeline) in the insurance sector (with FDI cap of 26 per cent) has provided more avenues to save to the customers along with dynamic returns and quality service. The share of this sector in total savings increased from 8 per cent in 1980 to 14 per cent in 2006. Further, the growth of the insurance business in India has resulted in employment generation on the one hand and provided a boost to the financial markets on the other.[16]

Booming Entertainment and Media Services

In this information-intensive age, media is a tool for dissemination of information, knowledge and forms of entertainment. Entertainment and Media Services comprise of television, films, radio, music, print media, live television and advertising. "There is a huge media explosion" in India. A Study conducted by FICCI-PWC in 2005 established that the Indian Media and entertainment industry currently pegged at Rs.35,300 crores is likely to touch Rs.83,740 crores by 2010. It has consistently out-performed the GDP growth rate year after year and is expected to grow at a compound annual growth rate of 19 per cent till 2010 and beyond. Inter alia, increasing incomes and rising consumer spending, technological innovations accompanied by liberal policy of the government permitting 100 per cent foreign equity in the film sector and advertising, 26 per cent in news related print media (editorial management must remain Indian), and 20 per cent FDI in FM radio, account for the double digit growth rate registered by this sector.

The fastest growing segment within the media industry is television. There was a single TV channel in 1990. In 2006, there were 300 channels. There are 108 million homes that have TV sets .The television industry has witnessed phenomenal growth and is expected to be worth Rs.42,700 crores in 2010, while it was just Rs.14,800 crores in 2005. So far as the print media is concerned, there are 60,413 newspapers in India. Total press readership stands at 222 millon. Radio, one of the most creative mediums for communication will be worth Rs.1200 crores by 2010. The recent grant by the central government for opening up of 300 FM stations is going to offer many opportunities for youngsters. The advertising industry is pegged at Rs.16,000 crores. All these facts and figures point out that there is a media revolution going on in India.[17]

16. Since 1993, twelve new private sector banks have been set up.

17. *India Today Aspire,* 2006: 12-29.

Conclusion

It is quite obvious from the foregoing discussion that currently we have been experiencing a services boom in India. Undoubtedly, increasing affluence, changing consumption patterns, increasing demand for life style products, increasing urbanisation, growing middle class and a "burgeoning youth brigade"[18] have acted as a buffer for services growth in India. However, within the services sector, there are a wide array of unconventional services *viz.*, professional services, IT and ITES, telecom services, organised retail, eco-tourism, health tourism etc which are the main drivers of services sector growth, though conventional services like unorganised retail, real estate and entertainment services too are contributing tremendously to services growth.[19] As per the *Economic Survey (2006-07)*, "Services Sector growth has continued to be broad-based. Among, the three sub-sectors of services, 'trade, hotels, transport and communication services' have continued to boost the sector by growing at double-digit rates for the fourth successive year. Impressive progress in information technology (IT) and IT-enabled services, both rail and road traffic, and fast addition to existing stock of telephone connections, particularly mobiles, played a key role in such growth. Growth in financial services (comprising banking, insurance, real estate and business services), after dipping to 5.6 per cent in 2003-04 bounced back to 8.7 per cent in 2004-05 and 10.9 per cent in 2005-06. The momentum has been maintained with a growth of 11.1 per cent in 2006-07."

18. *The Economic Times* (2007), February 9.
19. Conventional services are the old services like unorganised retail, real estate etc. and unconventional services are new services like professional services, IT, ITES, financial services (ATMs, credit cards), telecom services (like cellular phones), health services (tele-medicine) tourism services (eco-tourism, health tourism) etc which have been noticed especially after the Liberalisation and globalisation of the economy in 1991.

References

Acharya, Shankar (2007). "India's Growth: Past and Future", Paper for presentation at the *Eighth Annual Global Development Conference of the Global Development Network.* January 14-16. Beijing.

Economic Times (2007). "Crazy Kiya Re", *ET Realty,* Feburary 9, p.2.

———. (2007). "Reality or Illusion", *ET Realty,* Feburary 2, p.4.

Financial Express (2007). "India Inc's Retail Play Gets Big and Real", *Financial Express,* January 15, p.8.

———. (2007). "Serving the Nation", *Financial Express,* February, p.3

———. (2007). "Growth Drivers", *Financial Express,* March 15.

Government of India (2006-07). *Economic Survey.* New Delhi: Ministry of Finance.

———. (2006). *Towards Faster and More Inclusive Growth: An Approach to the 11th Five Year Plan.* June 14, pp.35-38. New Delhi: Planning Commission.

Hindustan Times (2007). "Tech firms Show Numbers To Keep Tax Breaks", *Hindustan Times,* Feburary 21, p.26.

India Today Aspire (2006). "The Media Revolution". *India Today Aspire.* pp.12-14.

Joshi, Seema (2004). "Tertiary Sector- Driven Growth in India: Impact on Employment and Poverty", *Economic and Political Weekly* 39(37): 4175-4178. Sept 11-17.

———. (2006a). "From Conventional to New Services: Broadened Scope of Tertiary Sector", *Indian Journal of labour Economics* 49(2): 321-335, April-June.

———.(2006b). "Employment Generation Potential in the Organised Retail Sector in Urban Areas", *Nagarlok,* September-December.

Lahiri, Ashok K. (2006). "Financial Sector Reforms in India: Steps and Effects on the International Financial System", Presentation made in the Opening Plenary Session at the *Program of Seminars.* Singapore. September 16.

Maheshwari, Shruti (2006). "The Media Revolution", *India Today Aspire,* November.

Mitra, Arup (2008). "Tertiary Sector Growth: Issues and Facts", *Artha Beekshan,* Vol. 16(4), March.

Naidu, Rajesh (2007). "Milk the Potential", *Financial Express: FE Investor,* February 25. p.13.

Ramasubramanian, R. (2006). "FDI in Retail: Major Arguments", *Mainstream,* February, pp.10-16.

Times of India (2007). "200 m Phones and Growing", *Times of India,* Feburary 18, p.1.

———.(2007). "Services Exports may touch $311 b by 2012", *Times of India,* April 16, p.24

Vaish, Nandi (2007). "No Room for Hospitality" *India Today,* January 1, p.46.

http://www.ibef.org/industry/tourismhospitality.aspx.p.1-3.

8

GATS, Indian Services Sector and Trade

Introduction

The General Agreement on Trade in Services (GATS) was one of the major areas of the General Agreement on Tariffs and Trade (GATT) in the Uruguay Round, which concluded in Geneva on Dec. 15, 1993. One of the important objectives of GATS is to promote trade in services through progressive liberalisation and enhancing the participation of developing countries in it. The developed countries account for major share in service exports (approximately 80 per cent) in contrast to developing countries who despite their advantageous position in producing cheaper services fail to reap the maximum benefits because of a plethora of tariff and non-tariff barriers on trade. In this context, the role of GATS becomes crucial for shaping the future course of world trade as it has brought services sector trade under its ambit.

In view of the ongoing 'service revolution' in our economy, the vast growth potential of service exports and also because of a provision of the multilateral framcwork for international trade in services under GATS, it is pertinent to examine the following questions:

a) What is the significance of trade in services?

b) What are the modes of service transaction available under GATS?

c) What is the current position of India in commercial services exports *vis-a-vis* other South Asian countries and also in which sector/component of commercial services its comparative advantage is the highest? What are the potential areas of service trade?

d) What is the trade potential in health services?

An attempt has been made in this chapter to answer the first two questions, to start with. Next we examine the current position of India *vis-a-vis* some other South Asian Countries. This is followed by a discussion on the state of health services, health infrastructure and potential for trade in health services. Finally, we summarise the conclusions.

What is the Significance of Trade in Services?

Keeping the definitions of services in mind, we discuss here the question: What is the significance of trade in services? This question has assumed significance because of a number of reasons:

1. Traditionally speaking, services are considered to be non-tradeable because as compared to goods they are having certain distinct characteristics such as intangibility, non-storability, and also these are embodied in the person or thing in question. Some of them require physical proximity of the provider and the consumer (for example, the barber and client) as they have to be consumed as soon as they are produced. Therefore, they were outside the purview of GATT negotiations till its 8th Round. However, with the development in technology, it has become possible to store certain services such as information stored in a floppy–disc. Moreover, trade in services has become possible through four different modes of service delivery as have been specified in Part I of GATS. Technological advances (advent of internet services and consequent creation of a wide range of tradeable products varying from e-banking to telehealth to distance learning), satellite communication, relaxation and elimination of restrictions on entry of firms across countries and sectors and opening up of hitherto closed areas where the state was enjoying exclusive monopoly (e.g. telecommunication, power, insurance, banking, infrastructural services) have contributed to the growth of services trade in the more recent years.[1] Further, noticeable reduction in transport costs along with technological developments especially in Telecom and IT sectors have not only made many previously non-tradeable services (many professional

1. Chadha, 2003.

services like legal, accountancy and medical services, etc.) tradeable internationally but has further resulted in the creation of a new species of internationally traded services like data processing, software and heightened the scope of trade in previously traded services like international banking and insurance also.[2]

2. Even though presently we are having comfortable forex reserves, but in the past we faced forex crisis especially during first and second oil shocks (1973 & 1980 respectively) and also during economic crisis of 1991. Therefore, it would be in the interest of the economy if in addition to promoting our merchandise exports, we try out some alternative methods for earning forex through boosting export of services. This argument applies in case of all developing countries including India.
3. Both services and commodity producing sectors are inextricably linked through intersectoral linkages. In this modern era of globalisation and competition, the use of quality service inputs is becoming a pre-requirement for making our goods internationally competitive. The need for various complementary or producer services whether indigenous or imported, is bound to increase in the near future. Further 'splintering' of industrial activity will push up the growth of services by increasing the demand for service inputs for production of goods. Both Indian and foreign firms can provide the service inputs so required.
4. Some of the services are relatively cheaper in some countries than others due to difference in their factor endowments. Many developing countries like India have comparative advantage in providing certain kinds of services (e.g. professional, technical) at cheaper rates due to the availability of cheap labour. GATS has offered us immense opportunities to open up trade in those services. We should try to maximise our benefits by translating our export potentialities into actuality through appropriate policies.
5. Lastly, trade in services can prove to be instrumental in alleviating the acute problem of unemployment amongst the professional and technical personnel in countries like India by creating a

2. Ray, 1991.

demand for their services (doctors, nurses, teachers, computer experts, etc.) abroad.

What are the Modes of Service Transaction Available under GATS ?

The General Agreement on Trade in Services (GATS) is the first and only multilateral framework of principles and rules for governing international trade in services. Part I of GATS, containing the scope and definition of the agreement, defines trade in services as "the supply of a service from the territory of any other member; in the territory of one member to the service consumer of any other member; by a service supplier of one member, through commercial presence in the territory of any other member; and by a service supplier of one member, through presence of natural persons of a member in the territory of any other member."[3]

There are four modes specified in the agreement through which trade in services can materialise: Mode 1: cross-border supply (physical movement of provider or user not required e.g. e-banking, tele-medicine, distance learning, export of video cassettes of movies, music concerts, dance performances); Mode 2: consumption abroad (the movement of user to the provider e.g. foreign tourist visiting India and utilising hotel services, foreign patients utilising our health services and *vice versa*); Mode 3: Commercial presence (setting up of an establishment like a construction or an engineering firm offering construction or engineering services, FDI); Mode 4: the presence of natural persons (i.e. temporary movement of natural persons e.g. Indian professors, doctors visiting foreign universities as junior or senior fellows or engineers, consultants going abroad on short term basis).

As per the recent WTO estimates, Mode 3 accounts for the highest share in world trade in services (57 per cent) followed by Mode 1 (about 28 per cent), Mode 2 (14 per cent) and Mode 4 (1 per cent) respectively.

---

3. Mukherjee, 1995.

Table 8.1

Modes of Service Transaction Available under GATS

Modes of Service Transaction	*Example*	*Value of World Trade in Services* (2005)*
Mode 1: Cross Border Supply	Physical movement of provider or user not required e.g. IT and e-banking, telemedicine, distance learning, export of video cassettes of movies, music conerts, dance performances, etc.	28 per cent
Mode 2: Consumption Abroad	The movement of user to provider e.g. eco–tourism, medical tourism, etc.	14 per cent
Mode 3: Commercial Presence	Setting up of an establishment like a construction or an engineering firm offering construction or engineering services, FDI in services.	57 per cent
Mode 4: Movement of Natural Persons	Temporary movement of natural persons e.g. Indian professors, doctors visiting foreign universities as junior or senior fellows or engineers, consultants going abroad on short-term basis.	1 per cent

Note : *: WTO.

What is the Current Position of India in Services Trade *vis-a-vis* other Countries of South Asian Region and What are the Potential Areas of Services Trade?

After having discussed the significance of service trade for India in particular and developing countries in general and modes of services delivery available under GATS, we now examine the growth of the commercial services exports in India *vis-a-vis* some other countries[4] of the South Asian region. It is quite evident from Table 8.2 that the five South Asian countries, namely Bangladesh, India, Nepal, Pakistan, and Sri Lanka have witnessed a major structural change over the last two decades. In the countries of the region, the share of services in overall

4. Also see Chadha, 2003.

GDP registered an increase from 38 per cent in 1980 to 54 per cent in 2005, whereas the share of agriculture in GDP declined from 37 per cent to 19 per cent over the same period. India, Sri Lanka and Nepal have shown relatively sharp changes in their production structure as compared to other countries. But one thing is quite obvious from Table 8.2, that it is the services sector which has emerged as the dominant sector in the four countries of South Asia, with the exception of Nepal.

Table 8.2

Structure of GDP in South Asian Countries

(Percentage Share in GDP)

	Countries	Agriculture			Industry			Services		
		1980	1990	2005	1980	1990	2005	1980	1990	2005
1.	Bangladesh	34	30	20	24	21	27	42	48	53
2.	India	38	31.0	18	26	28	27	36.0	41	54
3.	Nepal	62	52	38	12	16	21	26	32	41
4.	Pakistan	30.6	25.6	22	25.6	25.7	25	43.8	48.7	53
5.	Sri Lanka	26.6	22.3	17	27.2	29.2	26	46.2	48.5	57
	South Asia	37.0	31.0	19	26.0	27.0	27	38.0	43.0	54

Source: World Bank. *World Development Indicators*, Various Issues.

It can be observed from the data given in Table 8.3 that high income economies account for more than 80 per cent of total exports of commercial services and the remaining is accounted for by the low income and middle–income countries. India's share in export of commercial services is 92 per cent of exports originating from South Asia.

So far as the share of exports of commercial services in total world exports (merchandise and commercial services) is concerned, it hovered around 19 per cent on an average during the TE 2003-05 (See Table 8.4). The similar share of four South Asian Countries was 30 per cent followed by shares of High Income countries (20.8 per cent), Low and Middle-income countries (14 per cent) respectively during the corresponding triennium. Amongst the South Asian countries, India's share was the highest followed by that of Nepal, Sri Lanka, Pakistan and Bangladesh. Within the South Asian region, the share of transport in commercial service exports is the lowest in Nepal (at 11 per cent) followed by India (12.5 per cent), whereas the share of other services is the highest in India (at 71.1 per cent) and the share of travel in commercial services exports is the lowest in Pakistan (9.2 per cent) amongst the five countries of South Asia during the TE 2003-05.

Table 8.3

Exports of Commercial Services from Major Economies of the World: A Comparison

(US$ mn)

Region/Economy	*1980*	*1990*	*2000*	*2005*	*Average (2003-05)*
Low and Middle Income Countries	64991	102929	261149	495951	406941.7 (19.1)
High Income Countries	327151	647432	1169694	1962711	1719500.3 (80.9)
World	392155	750361	1430843	2459852	2126520.3
South Asia	4177	6816	20908	60989	44782.3
Bangladesh	163	296	283	472	430
India	2949	4610	17670	56094	40258.3
Nepal	127	166	410	271	309.7
Pakistan	617	1218	1284	2042	1738
Sri Lanka	231	425	915	1519	1470.3

Note: Figures in the parentheses indicate the shares of low & middle income and high income economies in the world trade of commercial services.

Source: World Bank, *World Development Indicators*, Various Issues

Table 8.5 shows that there is only one component of commercial services i.e. other services where the two South Asian Countries *viz.*, India and Bangladesh are having revealed comparative advantage (RCA) in exports. India is having a clear cut RCA over the other three countries in the exports of other services. However, in travel and transport exports it is having comparative disadvantage. Therefore, former constituent of commercial services, i.e., other services is indeed a potential area of services trade.

Table 8.4

Proportion of Commercial Services in Total Exports and their Components in Commercial Service Exports in TE 2003-2005

(in Per cent)

Region/Economy	*ECS in TE*	*ST in CSE*	*STra in CSE*	*SOS in CSE*
Low and Middle Income Countries	14	23.9	45.6	30.6
High Income Countries	20.8	23.6	24.7	52.6
World	19	23.6	29.0	48.1
South Asia	30	19.7	16.4	63.9
Bangladesh	5.02	20.1	15.0	64.9
India	34.8	12.5	15.4	71.1
Nepal	29.1	11	59.7	29.3
Pakistan	11.2	54.5	9.2	36.3
Sri Lanka	20.4	42.1	31.0	26.9

Note: 1. (a) ECS in TE stands for export of commercial services in total exports (merchandise+CSE)

(b) ST in CSE implies share of transport in commercial services exports

(c) STra in CSE implies share of travel in commercial services exports

(d) SOS in CSE stand for share of other services in commercial services exports

2. Commercial services comprise of transport, travel, other commercial services.

3. Other commercial services include such activities as insurance and financial services, international telecommunications, and postal and courier services, computer data, news–related service, transactions between residents and non-residents, construction services, royalities and license fees, miscellaneous business, professional, and technical services, and personal, cultural, and recreational services.

Source: World Bank. *World Development Indicators*, Various Issues

One of the important methods to tap the potential of this sector is to allow more FDI (which is addressed under Mode 3, commercial presence) in various sub-sectors of other services like, health, education, financial, insurance and telecommunication services. Commercial presence of a legal entity in the host country having its roots in the home country can be justified on the ground that foreign investors will bring in not only capital but also technology and would thereby contribute to the growth and modernisation of many services. Besides, this can prove to be beneficial for employment generation. Further, supply of quality service inputs to manufacturing sector due to 'splintering' of industrial activity would enhance international competitiveness of our products and thereby would help in building up forex reserves and maintenance of surplus on current account of BoPs (the phenomenon which we have experienced only thrice in the post-independence era). Moreover, even though the share of the temporary movement of natural persons covered under Mode 4 of GATS is the lowest in the world trade of services, but if encouraged in case of professional and technical services like educational, health, legal, accounting, architecture and design, construction and engineering it can go a long way in improving the quality of human resources so essential for economic development.

Table 8.5

RCA in Commercial Services and its Three Components in Major Regions/Economies of the World in TE 2003-2005

Region/Economy	*CS*	*TS*	*TraS*	*OS*
Low and Middle Income Countries	0.7	1.0	1.6	0.6
High Income Countries	1.1	1.0	0.9	1.1
South Asia	1.6	0.8	0.6	1.3
Bangladesh	0.3	0.9	0.5	1.4
India	1.8	0.5	0.5	1.5
Nepal	1.5	0.5	2.1	0.6
Pakistan	0.6	2.3	0.3	0.8
Sri Lanka	1.1	1.8	1.1	0.6

Note: 1) RCA stands for revealed comparative advantage, CS for commercial sevices, TS for transport services, TraS for travelservices and OS for other services respectively.

2) RCA is the ratio of two different ratios. The numerator is the ratio of export of commercial services of the region/country to its total exports (merchandise+CS). The denominator is the ratio of world export of CS to world exports.

3) In case of components of CS, the numerator is the ratio of export of a component of commercial services (TS/TraS/OS) of the region/country to its total exports of CS. The denominator remains the same for each region/country and is the ratio of world export of that particular component to world exports of CS.

4) RCA>1 implies comparative advantage RCA<1 implies absence of comparative advantage.

5) RCA has been calculated following Chadha, 2003.

Source: World Bank. *World Development Indicators*, Various Issues

Trade Potential in Health Services

Having discussed the growth of commercial services in India *vis-a-vis* other South Asian countries and identifying the potential comparative advantage of India in exporting 'other services' comprising among other services health services also, we now turn to examine the health status of India's population and the state of health infrastructure in our economy so that gaps if any can be filled up through encouraging trade in such services.

Health Policy and Health Status[5]

The first formal healthcare policy for India was laid out by the Bhore Committee Report (1946). Despite the fact that it was adopted by the Government of India, its recommendations couldn't be implemented fully due to financial stringency of the central government. In the formulation of the National Health Policy, the state governments are also involved as the bulk of expenditures on health sector is incurred by them.

The importance of development of health services and health infrastructure has been duly recognised in the various five year plans in India. A New Policy "Health for all by 2000 AD" (1977) had announced a long-term objective of population stabilisation by bringing down net reproduction rate to 1 by 1995. Since this goal could not be achieved, the National Health Policy (1983) outlined in the Eighth Five-Year Plan reiterated the same goal. Despite two decades of governmental emphasis on access to health services by all as India also being a signatory to on access to health services by all as India also being a signatory to Alma-Ata Declaration (1978), we are nowhere near this goal. The reiteration of the above-mentioned goal in New Health Policy (1983) and consequent larger allocations for health account one can observe the rise in health expenditure from 0.8 per cent of GDP in 1980-81 to 0.92 per cent in 1989-90 (i.e. during pre-reform period). During the post-reform period, the expenditure incurred on health sector rose from 0.83 per cent of GDP in 1991-92 to 0.89 per cent in 1992-93 and settled down at 0.76 per cent of GDP in 1997-98. Government is contributing just 0.9 per cent of GDP to the health sector at present. In New Health Policy, 2001,

5. This section is based on Joshi (2003) and also see Joshi (2006).

there is a proposal to raise it to 2 per cent of GDP by 2010. The current annual per capita public health expenditure in the country is just about Rs. 200. Besides the reach and quality of public health services has been below the desirable levels.

Table 8.6

Public Health Expenditure in India (1980-81 to 2003)

Year	*Health (in Rs. crore)*
Pre-Reform Period	
1980-81	943 (0.8)
1989-90	3767 (0.92)
1990-91	4508 (0.88)
Post-Reform Period	
1991-92	4888 (0.83)
1992-93	5621 (0.89)
1993-94	6218 (0.79)
1994-95	6920 (0.73)
1995-96	7880 (0-.73)
1996-97	9231 (0.72)
1997-98	10544 (0.76)
2000	(0.9)*
2003	1.2**

Note: Figures in parentheses indicate percentage to GDP.

*: Figures for the year 2000 are given from UNDP, *Human Development Report 2003*, p.256.

**: Figures for the year 2003 are given from UNDP, *Human Development Report 2006*, p.303.

Source: Central Statistical Organisation, *Selected Socio-Economic Statistics for India*, 2000, Department of Statistics, Government of India, p.64.

It is clear from the above Table that in spite of the fact that human development is at the core of our planning and reforms, yet the allocations made to the social sector as a whole and particularly to health have not only been low during the post-reform period but these have also been declining due to lack of political commitment on the part of governments which is crucial for achieveing the goal of human development.

Since the 1980s, notable improvements have taken place in India on some of the health indicators like life expectancy (63.7 years in 2002) and infant mortality rate (67 per thousand live births in 2002), mainly as a result of large-scale government programmes. But we have still long way to go to achieve 'health for all' as our performance compares poorly with that of the USA and even Sri Lanka in this regard. This is clear from the date given in Table 8.7 below.

Table 8.7

Basic Health Indicators

Indicator	*USA*	*India*	*Sri Lanka*	*Bangladesh*	*Pakistan*
Life Expectancy (2004)	77.5	63.6	74.3	63.3	63.4
Infant Mortality Rate (per 1,000 live births), 2004	7	62	12	56	80
Under-five mortality Rate (per 1,000 live births), 2004	8	85	14	77	101
Maternal Mortality Rate Ratio Adjusted (per 100,000 live births), 2000	17	540	92	380	500

Source: UNDP. *Human Development Report*, 2006. pp.315-317

The high infant mortality rate, high child mortality rate and high MMR reflect the poor state of public health of people, inadequate medical attention during pregnancy and at the time of child birth and also poor post-natal care. The following are the factors causing high infant mortality rate (IMR) and crude mortality rate (CMR).

(a) Poor Child and Maternal Health Care

The health status of vast majority of population continues to remain poor despite more than 10 years of reforms. As per *Human Development Report 2006*, 20 per cent population of India was undernourished as against Indonesia's 6 per cent and China's 12 per cent. During 1996-2004, the proportion of low birth weight infants was 30 per cent in India. The maternal mortality rate (MMR) per 1,00,000 live births, between 1990 and 1998, was estimated to be around 410 as against 65 per 1,00,000 live births in China. In 2004, MMR was 540 for China just 56 per 1,00,000 live births. In 1998-99 (by which eight years of reforms had been completed), 58 per cent of population (in the age group of 12-23 years) was not immunised. Besides, 35 per cent of India's population was not having access to essential drugs and 12 per cent of the population was not using improved water sources in 1999 and 14 per cent in 2004 (IGIDR, 2000; UNDP, 2001; 2002; 2006).

(b) Availability of Health Services and Infrastructure

The Tables given below (Table 8.8, 8.9 and 8.10) reflect the availability of health services and infrastructure in the country over 1971-1997/1999 period. No doubt the availability of health services and health infrastructure have improved over the period, yet the number of health personnel and quantity of health infrastructure falls short of the requirement. Still more appropriate and significant issue involved is not the quantity but the quality of both of these.

It is worth pointing out here that although social sector services are the responsibility of the states, yet in 1998 substantial proportion of population in India was not able to access health services. This is evident from the fact that medical professional assistance at the time of child birth was not available to 57.5 per cent of population in 1998-1999. The data about percentage distribution of deaths by type of medical attention received before death is also disturbing. It reveals that during the period of reforms this percentage increased from 12.4 per cent in 1991 to 16.7 per cent in 1996 in rural areas, so far as institutional attention was concerned. In urban areas, it increased from 31.3 per cent in 1991 to 35.7 per cent in 1996. It is important to point out here that at 16.7 per cent in rural areas and 35.7 per cent in urban areas, more or less 83 per cent of rural population and 64 per cent of urban population did not have access to institutional assistance before death (CSO, 2000). Besides, there was relative shortage of hospitals, dispensaries and hospital beds as is evident from the Table 8.10. The availability of these services is much worse in rural areas.

Table 8.8

Sources of High Infant, Child and Maternal Mortality Rate

Children 12-23 months without immunisation* (1998-99)	58
No access to improved water source (2000)**	16
No access to improved sanitation (2000)**	72
No institutional assistance at the time of birth (1996)***	74.8

Source: *: IGIDR. *India Development Report 2002.*

**: UNDP, *Human Development Report 2003.*

***: CSO. *Selected Socio-Economic Statistics 2000.*

Table 8.9

Selected Indicators of Health Services

No. of	*1971*	*1981*	*1991*	*1999*
Personnel per 100,000 population				
Doctors	27	39	47	52
Nurses	14	21	40	64
Auxillary Nurse/Midwives	5	10	18	32
Health Visitors	·0.81	1.35	2.03	2.61

Source: Central Statistical Organisation. *Selected Socio-Economic Statistics for India 2000.* Department of Statistics, Government of India. p.64.

Table 8.10

Selectecd Indicators of Health Infrastucture

Indicators	*1971*	*1981*	*1991*	*1997*
No. of Beds all types (per 100,000 of population)	64.0	83.0	95.0	93.0
No. of Hospitals	3862	6804	11174	15188
No. of Dispensaries	9087	16751	27431	25670
No. of Public Health Centres	5112	5740	20450	21536*

Note : Figures are for 1995.

Source: Central Statistical Organisation, *Selected Socio-Economic Statistics for India*, 2000, Department of Statistics, Government of India, p.64.

There has been an increase in HIV/AIDS cases in India during the reform period. This poses a challenge for the health planners as well as service providers. The seriousness of this epidemic can be judged from the fact that in 1997, out of total AIDS cases of 4.1 million reported in South Asia in the age group of 0-49 years, India accounted for as many as 97 per cent of these cases. Within India great regional disparities existed across different regions. Three quarters of AIDS cases were reported in three states, namely, Maharashtra, Tamil Nadu and Manipur (Mahbub ul Haq Human Development Centre, 2001). In addition to this new disease, there has been re-emergence of certain old diseases like TB, Malaria and Dengue at a faster pace.

The above discussion clearly indicates that in India not only quantity of health services and infrastructure but the quality of both is poor. Evidence also indicates that even though private practice by government doctors is not permitted, yet it is increasing (Bhat, 1995). Still another noticeable recent trend (Gupta, Goldar and Mitra, 1998) is that government doctors attracted by better pay package and working conditions are resigning and joining the private sector i.e. responding rationally to market signals. However, this is depriving the government sector of its cream. It has been rightly pointed out in a study (1998) that if government doctors can get short-term assignments abroad in a relatively easy manner, they may not take this extreme decision of leaving the public sector.

Given this scenario, it is our hunch that opening up of the health sector for foreign trade would be beneficial for improving the quantity and quality of health sevices and may create an internal brain drain (Mukhopadhyay, 2002).

GATS and Health Services: Gains and Constraints

Trade in health services is covered in the GATS under business services (professional services); health related social services.

In the case of health services, four modes of supply of services specified under GATS correspond to:

1. Tele-medicine services (cross-border supply),
2. A patient traveling abroad for treatment (Consumption abroad),
3. A foreign maintenance organisation. operating in another country (commercial presence); and
4. Health professionals working abroad (movement of natural persons).[6]

India has made GATS commitments in 6 out of 12 services sectors, *viz.* 1,2,3,7 and 8 and the market access has been permitted in this sector with foreign equity ceiling of 51 per cent. There are no limitations on national treatment, implying foreign investor would be treated at par with domestic investor. Health services have been covered under Sectors 1 and 8. Since GATS operates *via* specific commitments, and in the South-East Asian Region, India is the only country which has made some commitments in only one sub-sector, i.e., hospital

6. Gupta, Goldar and Mitra (1998).

services (sector 8). India has made no commitments in case of three health related professional services (sector 1) *viz.*, medical and dental services (A.h), veterinary services (A.i) and services provided by midwives, nurses, physiotherapists and paramedical staff (A.j).[7]

The next question which needs further probing is that out of the above-mentioned four modes which one is more relevant for India. What are the possible gains and constraints associated with them? Studies reveal that in addition to Mode 1 and 2 the last two modes 3 and 4 are also very relevant for us.

Table 8.11

Trade in Health Services: Benefits/Gains and Constraints for India

	Modes of Trade in Health Services	*Expected Gains*	*Constraints*
1.	Telehealth sevices (e.g. telemedicines, telepathalogy, teleradiology, telepsychiatry)	• Greater exchange of information • Lower costs and quick access to information • Bridging up rural-urban gap • Geography would be history	• Infrastructural bottlenecks • Shortage of computer savvy healthcare personnel • Lack of training facilities w.r.t. the application of ICT in medicine • Virtually no exposure to the application of ICT in curriculam of medical colleges • Financial constraints to access internet • Lack of regulatory framework to ensure the quality and content of health services 2.
	Medical tourism (movement of patients to avail assistance)	• Medical expertise • FOREX earnings • Better infrastructure	• Lack of portability of health insurance • Against the medical principle of equity
3.	Mode 3: FDI (e.g. joint ventures, alliances, management tie-ups in health sector)	• Upgradation, expansion and modernisation of health infrastructure • Upgradation of standards in hospitals	• Internal brain drain (shift of medical personnel from govt to private hospitals) • Expensive health

(contd...)

7. Chadha (2003).

(...contd...)

		• Better management practices • Employment generation • Less burden on govt. resources, which can be be diverted to improve public sector facilities	services due to commercialisation • Two-tier structure of service supply • Against the principle of equity and may lead to social distress
4.	Temporary Movement of natural persons (e.g. doctors, specialists, nurses, paramedics, midwives, technician, consultants, health management personnel, other skilled and trained professionals)	• Skill renewal • Information exchange • Increase in productivity • Greater exposure and experience with modern technology will impart value to Indian medico-staff • Gain due to networking abroad • Increase in remittances	• External brain drain for a short span • Economic needs requirement • Discriminatory licensing • Accredition • Recognition of foreign professional qualifications • Nationality and residency requirements • Immigration regulations • Discriminatory regulation of fees and expenses • Might lead to trafficking if host country does not ensure respect for its labour and/or rights • Might be used as tool for establishing a permanent residence in host country • Might be in conflict with immigration policies

Sources: Based on:

1. Kaufmann, Chadha and Winters, 2003.
2. Mukhopadhyay, 2002.
3. Gupta and Goldar, 2001.
4. Gupta, Goldar and Mitra, 1998.
5. Chanda, 2000.
6. *http:/www.wa.gov.au/tiac/health/health-04.htm*
7. *http://www. spsood.com/telemedicineinindia.htm*
8. *http://www.thamburaj.com/telemedicine.htm*
9. Authors views.

So far as telemedicine services (Mode 1) are concerned they are becoming an integral part of health care services in India. Though these are still in an embryonic stage yet there is no denial of the fact that there has been exchange of information on health and medicines through internet. Telemedicine has been identified as one of the thrust areas for the development of the country by the Ministry of Communication and Information Technology, Government of India. "India can be classified as one of the countries with a potential to reap from almost all the applications of telemedicine."[8] Even exchange of patients (Mode 2) carries vast forex earning potential, keeping in view India's comparative advantage in providing health services at cheap rates especially in South Asian region.[9] Not only this, another potential area in this regard is old-age nursing homes. In Organization for Economic Cooperation and Development (OECD) countries, there has been substantial increase in the number of old and disabled people who need nursing care for a prolonged period. As per United Nations and WHO estimate (1998), if only 3 per cent of the 100 million elderly persons living in OECD countries retired to developing countries, they would bring with them US$ 30-50 billion annually in personal consumption and $ 10-15 in medical expenditures. A major constraint to trade under Mode-2 is the lack of portability of health insurance e.g. in the US non-coverage of services delivered abroad under medicare, in OECD lack of long-term portability of health coverage and in some other countries extension of coverage abroad may be for a limited period of say, two or three months.[10]

It is likely that relaxation and gradual elimination of restriction on the entry of private/foreign firms (FDI in health services) would help to improve the capacity, quality and accessability of services in the private sector and might add to the supply of skilled personnel in the country. This mode can also help the other modes of supply like telemedicine as

8. *http://www. spsood.com/telemedicineinindia.htm*

9. Chadha (2003) gives an example in this regard. The cost of cardiovascular surgery package in Massachusetts General Hospital (Boston) is $ 47000, whereas in India's ISO-9000 certified Apollo Hospital (Chennai), it costs about $ 6000. Even in a low cost hospital in the United States named Christiana Hospital (Newark) it costs $ 28000. The corresponding figures for neurosurgery are about $ 42000, $ 3500 and $ 23000 respectively in the above-mentioned three hospitals.

10. ibid.

well as movement of patients and personnel across borders. But it is being apprehended that this can have adverse implication for the quality of service in the government hospitals. Therefore, studies emphasise that firstly, there should be greater emphasis on improvement of quality all around especially in the government hospitals which are visited by poorer sections. Secondly, to ensure quality and fairness, accredition of hospitals and introduction of regulatory norms need to be introduced. Thirdly, appropriate safegurds need to be introduced to ensure that obsolete technology is not passed onto Indian counterparts. Fourthly, there should not be glut of health services due to oversupply, and fifthly, both Indian and foreign establishments should not indulge in unfair trade practices (Gupta, Goldar and Mitra, 1997; Gupta and Goldar, 2001). Lastly, innovative methods need to be developed to prevent 'internal brain drain' i.e. shift of medico-staff from public to private hospitals (Chadha, 2003).[11]

Since India is having abundant supply of labour willing to move temporarily to work and as pointed out earlier also that the share of TMNP is nearly insignificant at 1 per cent, therefore, this is the potential area for developing trade in services. We may be loser in the sense that there may be 'external brain drain' for a short span due to TMNPs (as we will have to part with our skilled persons) but there may be 'internal brain gain' in the medium and long term. TMNPs to advanced countries would impart value to Indian medico-staff through their exposure to and experience with the modern technology as well as modern medical facilities available in advanced countries around the globe and help raising their productivity. Besides, we would stand to gain due to establishment of networking abroad by these persons, remittances and also through skill renewal and information exchange.[12] The scope for expanding trade under Mode 4 depends on how effectively the potential impediments under this mode of delivery are overcome. There are many barriers to the movement of individual

11. Chadha (2003). He suggests that special taxes should be imposed on patients who could afford to pay higher prices for either jumping the queue of waitlist or getting luxurious stay while under treatment. Revenue thus generated can be used for the upkeep of the public sector hospitals through enabling them to retain their medico-staff with them and yet provide "reasonable quality."

12. For this sub-section see, Gupta *et al.*, 1998 and Kaufmann *et al.*, 2003.

service providers. Explicit quotas and/or economic needs tests, numerous formalities associated with the securing of a visa, qualification and licensing requirements and the regulation of professional bodies are some of the major barriers.[13]

The results of an exclusive study conducted by Kaufman, Chadha and Winters (2003) to examine whether the GATS framework can accommodate health services and, in particular, the temporary movement of health workers or not, reveals that TMNPs under GATS is a complex and not completely clarified issue. It is being apprehended that temporary movement can be used as a tool for establishing permanent residence in host country and might conflict with immigration policies. The study suggested the introduction of a GATS visa which should be further examined in this context.

Conclusions

In view of the ongoing 'service revolution' in our economy, its vast export growth potential and also because of a provision of the multilateral framework for trade in services under GATS, it is pertinent to develop/liberalise this sector further by utilising various modes of service delivery specified in Part I of GATS for promoting world trade in this sector. Among various kinds of services, health related services constitute a major potential area for growth in services trade. India can gain enormously through opening up of this sector through permitting of FDI (under commercial presence, Mode 3), exchange of patients (under consumption abroad, Mode 2) and exchange of medical professionals, etc. (under temporary movement of natural persons i.e TMNPs under Mode 4). However, appropriate safeguard measures need to be undertaken to maintain a balance between equity and efficiency, public and private systems to ensure that the basic health services are supplied to weaker/vulnerable sections at affordable prices. Further, liberalisation of trade in services should be accompanied by liberalisation in agriculture and manufacturing sectors too, as isolated growth of services is not desirable from the viewpoint of long-term economic growth and its sustainability.[14]

---

13. Chadha, 2003.

14. Complementarity of the three sectors has been emphasised in Joshi (2004).

References

Bhat, Ramesh (1995). *The Private/Public Mix in Health Care in India.* Washington DC: International Health Policy Programme.

Bhagwati, J.N. (1984). "Splintering and Disembodiment of Services and Developing Nations", *The World Economy* 7(2): 133-34.

Central Statistical Organisation (2000). *Selected Socio-Economic Statistics for India 2000.* Department of Statistics, Ministry of Finance, Government of India.

Chadha, Rajesh (2003). *Competitiveness of Service Sectors in South Asia: Role and Implications of GATS.* Jaipur: CUTS Centre for International Trade, Economics and Environment.

Chanda, Rupa (2000). "GATS and its Implications for Developing Countries: Key Issues and Concerns", *UN/Discussion Paper of the United Nations Department of Economic and Social Affairs* (UN/DESA), Discussion Paper No. 25. November.

Giarini, Orio (1987). *The Emerging Service Economy.* Oxford: Peragamon Press.

Gupta, Indrani and Bishwanath Goldar (2001). *Commercial Presence in the Health Sector Under GATS: A Case Study of India.* Delhi: IEG (Report submitted to WHO/SEARO).

Gupta, Indrani, Bishwanath Goldar and Arup Mitra (1998). "International Trade in Health Services: The Case of India", in *International Trade in Health Services: A Development Perspective.* Geneva: UN/WHO.

Hill, T.P. (1977). "On Goods and Services", *Review of Income and Wealth,* 4, December.

Indira Gandhi Institute for Development Research (1999). *India Development Report 1999-2000.* New Delhi: Oxford University Press.

———. (2002). *India Development Report.* New Delhi: Oxford University Press.

Joshi, Seema (2002). *India Development Report.* New Delhi: Oxford University Press.

———. (2004). "Tertiary Sector- Driven Growth in India: Impact on Employment and Poverty", *Economic and Political Weekly* 39(37). Sept 11-17.

———. (2004). "Human Development and Tertiary Employment in Developing Countries", *Indian Journal of Labour Economics* 47(4). Oct-Dec.

———. (2006). "Impact of Economic Reforms on Social Sector Expenditure in India", *Economic and Polirical Weekly* XLI(4). January 28-February 3.

Kaufmann, Christine Breining, Rajesh Chadha and L. Alan Winters (2003). *GATS and Temporary Movement of Natural Persons in the Health Sector.* A paper prepared for and supported partially by the European Commission, June 2.

Mahbub ul Haq Human Development Centre (2001). *Human Development in South Asia.* Oxford: Oxford University Press.

Marx, Karl (1909). "The Physiocrats to Adam Smith", *Das Capital.* C.H. Kerr and Co., Chicago, Vol.III.

Mukherjee, Neela (1995). *GATT Uruguay Round, Developing Countries and Trade in Services.* New Delhi: Vikas Publishing House Pvt. Ltd.

Mukhopadhyay, Sukumar (2002). "Globalisation and Indian Services Sector", *Economic and Political Weekly,* Oct. 5.

Ray, Alok (1991). "Trade in Services for Developing Countries in 1990s: Problems and Prospects", *Economic and Political Weekly,* March 2-9.

Sampson, Gary, P. and H. Snape Richard (1985). "Identifying the Issue in Trade in Services", *World Economy,* 2, June.

Smith, Adam (1910). *An Enquiry into the Nature and Causes of the Wealth of Nations*, Vol.II, Chap. III. Dent: London.

UNDP (2001). *Human Development Report*. New York: Oxford University Press.

———. (2002). *Human Development Report*. New York: Oxford University Press.

World Bank (Various Years). *World Development Indicators*. Various Issues

---

This chapter is based on "GATS, Indian Services Sector and Trade Potential in Health Services", in *International Conference on Services Management*. Conference Proceedings, IIMT (Institute for International Management and Technology), Haryana, India. 2005, pp.192-200.

Index

D

H

I

N

O

P

Q

R

S

T

U